Studs Terkel's
WORKING

A Teaching Guide

Studs Terkel's
WORKING

A Teaching Guide

RICK AYERS

Permission has been granted to reprint the following copyrighted material:

Excerpt by David Wild from *Rolling Stone* (July 8, 1999). © Straight Arrow Publishers, l.p. 1999.
Reprinted by permission.

Excerpt from *Hell's Angels* by Hunter S. Thompson. Reprinted by permission of Ballantine Books,
a division of Random House, Inc.

Excerpt from Kenneth L. Kann. *Comrades and Chicken Ranchers: The Story of a California Jewish
Community*. Copyright © 1993 by Kenneth L. Kann. Used by permission of the publisher,
Cornell University Press.

"I, Too" from *Collected Poems* by Langston Hughes © 1994 by the Estate of Langston Hughes.
Reprinted by permission of Alfred A. Knopf, a division of Random House, Inc.

Published in the United States by The New Press, New York, 2001
Distributed by W. W. Norton & Company, Inc., New York

LIBRARY OF CONGRESS CATALOGING-IN-PUBLICATION DATA

Ayers, Rick.
Studs Terkel's Working : a teaching guide / Rick Ayers.
p. cm.
ISBN 1-56584-626-5 (pbk.)
1. Terkel, Studs, 1912– Working. 2. Working class—United States—Studying and
teaching—Handbook, manuals, etc. I. Title.
HD8072.A94 2001
331.2'0973—dc21   00–055408

The New Press was established in 1990 as a not-for-profit alternative to the large,
commercial publishing houses currently dominating the book publishing industry. The New
Press operates in the public interest rather than for private gain, and is committed to
publishing, in innovative ways, works of educational, cultural, and community value
that are often deemed insufficiently profitable.

The New Press, 450 West 41st Street, 6th floor, New York, NY 10036

www.thenewpress.com

Designed by Mark Melnick

Printed in Canada

2 4 6 8 9 7 5 3 1

In memory of
HENRY MAYER

Contents

IV. RESOURCES

Acknowledgments

Curriculum development, at its best, is a cocreative and exciting process. While some teachers are famous for hoarding and hiding curriculum materials, most are delighted to share what they have found to work and which might help someone else. The ideas in this book are by no means mine alone. Studs Terkel, of course, was the inspiration for everything. He embodies the teacher and student, the mentor and friend. His endless energy keeps a hundred projects alive and his giant heart has room for hundreds of close friends.

I have dozens of students and colleagues to thank but can only mention a few here, people whose work was a direct contribution to the book. First is Dave Donahue, curriculum and instruction teacher at Mills College, who has given the discipline the dignity and professionalism it deserves. Then there is Sydney Lewis, another friend of Studs's and a great oral historian in her own right, who provided feedback, insights, and an e-mail pal I could complain to. Meredith McMonigle and Bill Pratt of Berkeley High School have used *Working* effectively in their experiential learning program and history classes. Craig Kridel of the University of South Carolina Museum of Education was wonderful and generous in sharing information on biography and oral history. Henry Mayer, an incredible historian and biographer from Berkeley, shared both wisdom and contacts. Kenneth Kann, another great oral historian, shared his work without hesitation. Laury Fischer of the Bay Area Writing Project has created a fantastic interview process curriculum which he shared generously, and which Berkeley High teacher Jeff Rapson passed on to me. My mentor and friend Conn Hallinan, a journalism teacher at the University of California at Santa Cruz, has not only taught me about the art of the interview but has spent long hours helping develop the ideas in and direction of this book. Therese Quinn of the University of Illinois at Chicago gave the work a good read and showed me what a teaching guide should look like. Elizabeth Wright of San Francisco shared her oral history experience. Cliff Mayotte of the Berkeley Repertory Theatre gladly shared his expertise on oral history and theatrical performance. John Ayers and Bill Ayers were always encouraging and wonderful brothers to bounce ideas off of, and John conducted the marvelous interview with Studs that is included in this volume. Thanks to the Library of Congress for permission to use materials in the Oral History Unit, and to the Oral History Association for permission to copy their guidelines and protocols. Ellen Reeves, Tim Roberts, and Barbara Chuang at The New Press helped me understand this new process. And Ilene Abrams, my best friend and life partner, was the best support of all.

Introduction

The notion of creating a teaching guide to *Working*, Studs Terkel's great chronicle of human lives, may seem absurd. After all, the book is simple and straightforward. It is an easy read, something you can take in as a whole or in parts.

But it is also an incredible tool, a launching pad for powerful classroom activities. Around the world, in grade schools, high schools, colleges, even adult schools, teachers are using *Working* as part of their curricula. Some books are meant to be received, passively; *Working* calls out for action, calls for you to see your life, your world, differently. It calls on you to investigate, to meet people, and to know them. Studs Terkel propels you into a whole new adventure: your life. He calls on you to question easy assumptions, to demand to know why things are the way they are.

So, in the course of creating this guide, I began to ask such questions. Why, for instance, do we create a teaching guide? I've always been annoyed at curriculum material which consists simply of "chapter questions." Every teacher creates such questions every day; do they really need someone else to come up with these for them?

Curriculum itself is a strange construct. Should it be a bag of tricks, of ready-to-use handouts? Is curriculum simply a text or some ideas about how to manipulate a text? Teaching is a complex process. It embodies encounters between teacher and student, among students, and often among teachers . . . usually with a text or other object as the point of attention.

Teaching is, ultimately, an exciting and creative intellectual activity, as is learning. We have constructed these roles as those of the "giver" and the "receiver," but we all know the best school experiences happen when such boundaries are all mixed up, when we are exploring together. Thinking about Studs Terkel's insights into the world of working, it occurs to me that anyone can "deliver content"—even a disembodied voice on a computer screen, in that frightening new invention we call "distance learning." But it takes a wonderful magician, a change agent, a musician of souls, to truly teach.

So, at its best, a teaching guide should be an intellectual challenge, a professional discussion with colleagues, and an invitation to branch off and create more. This guide is a collection of just such discussions in a small corner of the planet, with the teachers and students I have known and sought out. No doubt dozens of other guides, equally provocative, could be generated from other loci, from other teachers.

Many years ago in Chicago, I had the pleasure to be interviewed by, and to call as a friend, Studs Terkel. The wonderful thing about Studs was that he always made you feel that your life, your story, was the most important thing in the world. Leaning forward, his animated face working, nodding, laughing, seeking clarification, Studs was completely there. He never filled you up with himself; he wanted to know about you, what made you tick, what your core passion was. His genuine interest made people open up to him, even made people discover things about themselves that they had not realized before.

The good interviewer and documenter reflects back your story with more clarity than your original telling. If the interviewer is sloppy, selfish, or narrow, you will resent the story he tells and deny its truth. If he is Studs, you recognize its essential truth and begin to better understand yourself, and your life.

When my friends and I met Studs Terkel in 1963, we were a bunch of suburban high school rebels, living twenty miles west of Chicago. We sought freedom by turning our radio dials to the black music stations, WVON and WYNR—discovering the beat of Bo Diddley and the heart of Aretha Franklin. We also came across WFMT, Chicago's "fine arts" radio station. We would sit up with the funky and eclectic Midnight Special folk show on Saturday nights and listen to Studs Terkel interviews in the mornings.

One day we ventured down to the Loop to take a record album to the Midnight Special producer. As we sat in the WFMT studio, Studs came bustling out, distracted and busy, his hair flying, a sheaf of papers, notes, and records under his arm. In spite of all his hurry, though, he stopped and said, "Hello, you young people. What are you doing here?" Then he did his 100 percent focus thing, leaning over, then sitting down, to find out all about us. Soon he boiled down his search to a central question, one he came back to again and again in our years of acquaintance: "I wonder, though, about you bunch of suburban kids. You're supposed to be training to be bank managers, you're supposed to be practicing your swing at the country club. What made you come down here to Chicago? What made you dissatisfied with your world? What is making these kids from the suburbs go down south, go on picket lines? What makes you tick?"

We began to think differently about ourselves. We weren't just confused and bored and dissatisfied. We were a phenomenon! We were pioneers. We were interesting. You can't imagine what that means to a teenager.

Studs later interviewed my brother and me about our father and his experiences in the Depression. Those short segments made it into *Hard Times*. I recently learned that playwright Arthur Miller, another hero of ours from those years, told Studs that our segment seemed important to him and he had thought for some time about building a play around it. I was thrilled to think that, thanks to Studs Terkel, I almost went from obscure suburban teenager to subject of an Arthur Miller play.

Norm Pellegrini, program director at WFMT, captures this bundle of energy in a piece he did for Tony Parker's *Studs Terkel, A Life in Words*:

> He doesn't have a sense of self-importance that's in any way inflated at all—yet if anyone would be entitled to have it, surely it would be him because of his achievements. Such an ordinary looking little guy, and though I don't think he uses it consciously to get out of people what he's after, which is usually some expression of something they've never given thought to before, maybe that's part of the reason people feel at ease talking to him.

> With Studs it's question, question, question—and then
> the next question and the next. What does this person think?
> Why does he think it? What made him the person who thinks
> it? His curiosity is endless, and it's honest curiosity into how
> people are; it's never motivated by jealousy or envy. (p. 5)

Studs Terkel is legendary as an interviewer, but not in a way that
makes him untouchable. If anything, he exults in being eminently imi-
table. He has sparked an interest in oral history that has reached new
heights. Today, university departments and private companies are collecting oral histories. And Studs has been responsible for some of the
best experiences millions of children have had in school: interviewing
elders and others in their communities.

There are dozens of ways to go when making use of *Working*, and
teachers have tried them all. Study of the book can be the occasion for
school-to-work reflection, thinking about possible careers and choices.
It can invite ambitious interview projects. It can be a jumping-off point
for economic analysis, comparing the world of work in the United States
in 1970 with that of today. It serves well as a starting point for work in
ethics, poetics, history, biography, journalism, and social studies.

The whole idea of collecting testimony—verbal evidence—in order
to describe a historical period or a person's life did not begin with Studs
Terkel, of course. Early historians like Herodotus in the fifth century BCE
relied on interviews and testimony, some of which were reported verbatim. Plutarch wrote biographies based on interviews and oral accounts.

And, of course, biography and transcribed testimony are particularly
Western forms of expression. If Shakespeare launched the era of secular
humanism with his work at the beginning of the seventeenth century,
James Boswell's *Life of Samuel Johnson, LL.D.* in the mid-eighteenth
century gave the transcribed narrative the force of literature.

But other cultures and peoples have had their own ways of remembering, of allowing their voices to be carried on. Often this was done
through oral history such as the Griot traditions of Western Africa or
repeated stories of indigenous peoples in the Americas. Chinese written
family histories often trace stories back in some cases thousands of years.

Of course, on an individual level, all memory is flawed. What actually happened? What is the objective truth? I remember when we had a seventieth birthday party for my mother. Each sibling was to prepare a testimony of remembered moments. I recalled the time our parents had just purchased a new living room table and, during a history project, I managed to get glue on the table and ruin the finish. It was one of the only times I saw my mother cry. This stuck in my memory, vividly. But the strange thing is this: Two other siblings remembered the same incident, only in their versions, they were the ones doing the gluing, ruining the finish, and making my mother cry. Who did it? We can't really remember. But the feeling is real for each of us.

Is Studs Terkel's work oral history or journalism? He says that he uses perhaps 5 percent of the material on the tape recordings he makes. In fact, Studs Terkel is telling his story, the story of our times, letting the voices of others serve as the main text. His work has spawned great developments in both oral history and journalism.

Studs Terkel brought together a number of important elements to touch off the explosion of interest in oral history. He knew about a project begun in 1948 at Columbia University to interview the "great men," the elites, of U.S. history. His own political radicalism impelled him to seek the truth, and the history, from the common man and woman rather than from the elites. He had participated in the Federal Writers' Project, whose members interviewed survivors of slavery and other working peoples. He had access to new and more portable tape recorders. And he had his regular talk and interview show on WFMT.

Terkel has been criticized for his methodology—the casual and uneven approach to gathering testimony, the editing of interviews, the authorial voice in the selection and arrangement of interviews. But then, Terkel never claimed to be creating an archive. Taken for what it is, *Working* is an incredibly inspiring meditation on the world of labor, as well as on the nature of alienation and power. Staying out of the fray of academic one-upmanship, Studs Terkel encourages students to pore over his work, to criticize and react, to try it out themselves. That is what makes his work accessible and ultimately important for young people today.

In 1996, Studs talked about *Working* with Tony Parker (*Studs Terkel, A Life in Words*, p. 135):

Yeah, well, this was the big one—in concept, in popularity, in how many copies it's sold over the years. A million or more, so they tell me. Again, the idea was André's [Schiffrin], and this time I didn't need much persuading about it. It fit in mentally with an idea I'd had in my head a long while, one we've talked about before. You know, "Who built the pyramids?" [Here, he's referring to a poem by Brecht.] Ask anyone that question and they say something like, "Everybody knows who built the pyramids; it was the pharaohs, right?" Wrong. It was the pharaohs had the *idea* of building the pyramids, for their own aggrandizement, to try and immortalize themselves. They wanted to show generations to come what rich and powerful and splendid guys they were. But they didn't actually build the pyramids themselves: they got peasants and slaves to do the actual work. It was *they* who built the pyramids, not the pharaohs. And because there weren't such marvelous things as tape recorders those days, nobody ever went around among the builders and asked them what it was like, how they did what they did, how they got those massive stone blocks arranged the way they were. I put Bertolt Brecht at the beginning of the book, his lines on the same theme . . . :

In the evening when the Chinese wall was finished
Where did the masons go?

So let's say I took the book as an opportunity to redress an imbalance, OK? Do something in the present that would have been terrific if other people had done it for their own times in the past.

What did I mean by the dedication? What does it say? "For Jude Fawley; for Ida, who shares his vision; for Annie, who didn't." Yeah, well, Jude Fawley is the main character in Thomas Hardy's *Jude the Obscure*: he's not a well-educated guy, but all his life he has this thirst for knowledge and education. He believes people can better themselves by reading and study, even if they come from humble backgrounds.

Everybody is potentially university material; I suppose you could say that was his vision: he was an idealist. And Ida is my wife, and basically she's like that, she thinks that way too. "Annie,"—well, that was my mother. She's dead now, and I guess I was being unfair to her in putting that in about her. I think maybe she did share Jude's vision but in a different kind of a way.

I have organized this Teaching Guide to be as user-friendly as possible. It is not meant to be read front to back, of course, and many sections elaborate on ideas started in others.

In Section I, I include a number of teaching units and lesson plans that explore in depth different subjects inspired by *Working*. Many of these come from my own classroom and from ideas that have worked for other teachers.

Section II is a series of questions and suggested activities keyed to each of the "books" in *Working*. The questions are simply discussion points for classroom reflection. The activities have been suggested and tested by actual classroom practice and are inspired by something in each "book" but of course can be used with others as well. Some of these activities will be easily adapted to the more developed lesson plans in the teaching units of Section I.

Section III contains an interview of Studs Terkel by John Ayers conducted specifically for this book, as well as examples of the process of editing an interview, using Studs's own editing marks on the manuscript.

Section IV is a resource guide, followed by a bibliography.

As always, this teaching guide is a work in progress. Please send feedback and new ideas to me so that future editions may be as useful as possible. You can post your own responses, experiences, and lesson plans at the Web site www.workingguide.com. This is a place to share ideas and to foster dialogue with each other about the use of the book.

I

TEACHING UNITS

Interview Techniques

INTERVIEWING PEERS
Lesson Plan No. 1

OVERVIEW: One of the most important ways to use Studs Terkel's *Working* is to have students do their own interviewing while they are reading the book. Students become intensely aware of issues of oral history, point of view, and journalism and history as they dive into this project. The steps of this unit have been developed through collaboration with a number of teachers at the high school and university level in the San Francisco Bay Area.

Note that this unit, broken into four lesson plans, can take as many as 14 days (class periods) over three weeks. This is one of the strongest, hands-on ways to engage in the process of interviewing and oral history. It fits well with journalism, history, or English classes. Many classrooms have used variations of this unit to conduct particular investigations, talking to grandparents, Vietnam or World War II veterans, immigrants, school personnel, and others.

This first activity is also a great way to start a semester, allowing students to get to know each other while being introduced to interviewing issues. There are many caveats to interviewing that could be given up front, but I think it's better for students initially to have a relatively "raw" experience trying to do the interview. Then they can deduce lessons from it. Issues that often come up are the complexity in multiple points of view or "lenses" (the interviewee, the interviewer, the class), how to plan the interview, how to pursue follow-up questions, how to pay attention, and how to get to the core of a story.

Objectives for Students

- Meet classmates and create a community.
- Practice writing an autobiographical sketch.
- Practice interviewing, going beyond author's autobiographical sketch.
- Discuss and consider issues of multiple points of view in telling a story.

TIME: Two or three class periods.

MATERIALS: Student journals/notebooks.

PROCEDURE:

Step 1: Present an overview of the plans for the coming unit: "In the coming week, you will become familiar with interview techniques, starting with a small project and bridging to a large, ambitious project. The interview is the cornerstone of journalism, history, and cultural studies."

Step 2: *Autobiographical sketch.* Ask students to write a brief autobiographical sketch that would give a reader some idea about who they are, including their personal history and their specific interesting accomplishments or experiences (15 minutes).

Step 3: *Partners.* Say to students: "You have now each written an autobiographical sketch. This constitutes the first lens, the first way of looking at the subject of 'you.' Now we will move on to the second lens, the interviewer.

"Exchange your autobiography with one other person, someone you don't know. This person will be your interview partner. Read his/her autobiography. Begin to plan an interview with the other person (10–15 minutes)."

Remind students to take some notes, perhaps considering the following:

- What aspects of the autobiography do I want to pursue further?

- What do I think would be interesting to bring out about this person?
- What is the hole in the donut (i.e., what is something that your partner avoids talking about but which you think would be interesting to know more about)?
- What new story would you like to construct about this person?

Step 4: *Planning the interview* (homework for the next class). Tell students to begin to plan the interview with the answers to the questions above in mind. Have them write out six to ten questions. Tell them also to develop a potential follow-up question for each original question that asks the interviewee to extend that answer further. Six questions should turn into at least twelve.

Step 5: *The interview*. The interview should be conducted during class time. Encourage students to go outside or to another comfortable place. Allow about ten minutes for students to conduct both interviews. Remind them when time is half over so they can switch interviewer and interviewee roles. Keeping the interview time short for this exercise helps keep the students focused and interested; however, some teachers have found that students can sustain a longer peer interview, perhaps 30 to 40 minutes. Your call.

Give students the following advice before they begin: Make your subject comfortable. In later interviews you may want to use a tape recorder, but this time, have lots of blank paper and be ready to write fast, while at the same time maintaining a positive and friendly tone to the conversation. Most important, give your full attention to the other person. Don't just read off the questions. Show that person that you are genuinely interested, that you want to know more, that you find his/her life the most fascinating thing in the world. With this attitude, you will elicit much more interesting and thorough responses. While you are taking notes, be sure to write down other things you observe: how the person looks, his/her clothes, the things around you in the room, body language. Your notes on these things will make your writing stronger when you write up the interview.

Step 6: *Homework*. For homework, have students write up their interviews. Students may include their own observations and comments, either in the introduction or in interjected italicized comments through-out the interview. They should feel free to edit out extraneous comments and to choose the points they want to highlight. Tell them to be prepared to read aloud the interview/report to the class as well as to hand in a written version.

Step 7: *Reporting.* The next class should be devoted to reporting on the interview process. Discuss how the interviews went. Did students feel comfortable? Awkward? Did they feel they did a good job? Why or why not? Then, have students take turns introducing their partners by reading their interview to the class. After each report, ask the subject of the report if he/she felt it was accurate. Ask if he/she wants to add or clarify any-thing. This feedback offers an occasion for more discussion of interview techniques. You might also have students read a few sentences from the interview and then ad-lib an introduction.

Step 8: *Evaluation.* Now return to a whole-class discussion. Discuss how an autobiographical sketch offers one perspective on an individual while the interview shines through a second lens, refracting the light from the first lens. Finally, point out how the class's own understanding and interpretation of the interview actually becomes the third lens. What we learn is that the interview process identifies not an objective truth but such questions as: How can we construct stories that make sense of reality? What if the interviewer has one truth—one perspective on the subject that seems true—which the interviewee does not like or accept? How does the interviewer get things wrong? Why? Who gets to publish their version? What is the final truth?

PROFESSIONAL MODELS
Lesson Plan No. 2

OVERVIEW: Here students are introduced to interviews as gathered and reported by professional media today. They learn that it is not enough just to go out, ask questions, and take down answers. The problems they encountered in interviewing peers—how the personality and perspective of the interviewer intrude on the way an interview is reported—are treated as an issue of narrative that a strong interviewer can understand and control.

The following activities help students begin to examine the interview process more deeply. They put the technique Studs Terkel developed into the context of other ways that interviews are reported. During these readings, students further their discussion of point of view and the responsibility of the interviewer. They also begin to consider their own upcoming interview assignment—both who they might interview and what problems they will have while conducting the interview. Students in many classes will be reading parts of Studs Terkel's *Working* as they are studying work by other interviewers. The following activities will allow them to reflect on what he has achieved and its implications for cultural discourse today.

Objectives for Students

- Understand the role the interviewer's viewpoint plays in the interview.
- Recognize three distinct ways that interviews may be reported.
- Begin discussing and planning their own interviews.
- Read published interviews more critically.

TIME: Two to three days.

MATERIALS: Copies of two sample interviews are included here on pages 21–26, but feel free to choose your own models.

PROCEDURE:

Step 1: *Setting the stage.* Discuss with students how interviews are used for many different purposes. Most news stories are based on interviews, as are many feature stories. In addition, interviews are used to create oral histories. All kinds of interviews are found in books, newspapers, and magazines and are reported in different forms and formats.

During the upcoming examination of all these examples, students should think about their own upcoming interviews: Who would be interesting to interview? How can the interview be done in an interesting and engaging way?

Step 2: *Q & A.* The "question and answer," or "Q & A," format of interviewing is the simplest: the interview is simply transcribed and read raw or with minimal editing. Examples of this are found in many magazines (*Interview, Rolling Stone*, and *Playboy*) every month. They begin with a long introduction, sometimes a whole magazine page, describing the background of the interviewee, establishing the context for the interview, even describing the look of the location where the interview took place. After that, however, it is simply Q & A. Read the first part of a typical interview (hand out a sample—*Rolling Stone* interview with Trey Parker and Matt Stone on page 21–23—and read part together).

Step 3: *Reflection.* Prompt discussion with the following questions: What advantages or strengths do you find with this Q & A technique? (Some answers might be: It is an accurate report of the discussion; it allows for a minimum of editing.) What are some limitations? (The main one I've encountered is that you have to have a chatty subject, someone who is strong at painting word pictures, someone who is interesting and engaging. The magazines listed earlier mostly interview celebrities, usually media-savvy celebrities, so this Q & A format works well.)

Step 4: *New Journalism.* Consider another type of interview. Hand out copies of the excerpt from *Hell's Angels* by Hunter Thompson (copy on pp. 24–26). Read the first page or so aloud.

This type of interview report is known as "New Journalism." It began in the 1960s when young writers began to "question authority" and allowed the personal observations of the journalist to burst into the picture. Some say that Hunter Thompson revolutionized journalism when he started doing this personal type of reporting. Here we see one of his early pieces, from his book *Hell's Angels.* He is also famous for his profile of Nixon and his generation, called *Fear and Loathing in Las Vegas.* Like an actor breaking the "fourth wall" of the stage, Hunter Thompson rejects the formal and, in his view, phony distance and objectivity that traditional interviewers maintained. He allows himself to be part of the story and to express his full opinion on what is going on.

In addition to Hunter Thompson, some of the first practitioners of this type of writing were Tom Wolfe, Joan Didion, and Gay Talese. New Journalism is more tricky and difficult in execution than it first appears: you can talk about yourself and your own observations all you want, but these observations must help throw a light on your subject. Thus, New Journalism is not just self-indulgence and lazy writing. It is an honest and complex way to describe reality. Hunter Thompson wrote about his own drug experiences while following Nixon around the country, but ultimately he created a book about Nixon, not himself.

Step 5: *Reflection.* Prompt students: What is different about this interview? (Students should notice that the author reveals a great deal about himself, describes details about the subject, and allows himself to express his subjective self, his personal responses.) What are some strengths of this approach? (Some observations students have made: It allows the author to be more creative, to bring in more of his/her point of view; it can make the interview more engaging and interesting even if the interviewee is not chatty or a great raconteur.) What are some limitations? (Students often worry more here about the author distorting the reality of the interviewee.)

Step 6: *Studs Terkel Style.* The third way an interview might be reported is in what is appropriately known as the Studs Terkel style. (Read together the first few pages of the interview with mason Carl Murray Bates in *Working*, p. xlv.) In a Studs Terkel interview, you do not talk about yourself like the New Journalist would. You begin with a short introduction to set the scene, then you report the interview. But here is where the authorship, the view of the interviewer, comes in more strongly than in the Q & A format: you edit, severely edit, the interview. You take out all, or almost all, of your own questions. You cut and edit the responses to create a coherent narrative from the interviewee—a monologue, if you will.

Step 7: *Reflection.* Discuss the Terkel-Bates interview (*Working*, p. xlv) in more depth. What are some strengths of this approach? (Often students have talked about how a more coherent picture of the subject emerges when his interview is thus edited. In addition, if one coaxes a story out of a reluctant or inarticulate subject, it may be boring to read as Q & A but compelling in the Studs Terkel style.) What are some of the drawbacks? (Many express concern about the authenticity of the final product if there has been too much manipulation of the tape by the interviewer.) For more detail on the early work of Studs Terkel and the Federal Writers' Project, see Oral History, on page 36.

Step 8: *Homework* (optional). Ask students to find two interviews in a newspaper, book, or magazine. Be clear that you are looking for an interview, not a news story containing quotations. Ask students to bring in their sample interviews and share a number of them with the class. Have the class classify them in one of the three categories already discussed, or have them create a fourth or fifth category. Again, discuss the strengths and weaknesses of each format.

INTERVIEW ASSIGNMENT
Lesson Plan No. 3

OVERVIEW: Student journalism, and student research and investigation, is greatly strengthened when students begin to understand the many decisions that go into conducting a successful interview. One reason so many steps are necessary to prepare students to do an interview is that interviews look deceptively simple: You just go out and ask some questions, right? But high school newspapers are full of stories written with halfhearted commitment by the student author, with dull and clichéd responses, and with dull subject matter. These are stories destined to be read by three or four students, and of course the writer's parents.

Journalism (and the interview) is one social role that gives permission to—and actually invites—a young person to approach a total stranger and say, "I want to ask you all about your life." Like all humans, teenagers are intensely curious about others, but they are notoriously narcissistic and actually shy and hesitant about talking to strangers. The examples (on pp. 27–35) of interviews conducted by students (and others students will collect) model teenagers breaking out of their hesitation. While each one is flawed in one way or another, each shows a strong commitment to reaching out and learning something about others. Through interviewing, students learn about their world and recognize how to use certain powerful conventions to report what they have learned.

If your students are working on a particular class project—such as investigating grandparents or local activists or career options—they will find these interview reporting models helpful in establishing the format of their own reports when they are done.

Objectives for Students

- Strengthen powers of observation and description.
- Identify interview techniques used in sample student work.
- Reflect on and plan an interview.

TIME: Three to four days.

MATERIALS: Handouts of student interviews, Interview Project assignment handout (p. 15), notebooks/journals.

PROCEDURE:

Step 1: *Garden observation.* This step can be incorporated into the process however you see fit. If you have other assignments that are designed to help students with observation skills and with writing about concrete things, you may skip this. I got this idea from educator Eliot Wigginton. First, the class discusses what makes writing powerful. I emphasize the importance of concrete observation. (It is a good idea to read an excerpt here from, say, John McPhee, who does fabulous reporting and nature writing.) Gathering concrete details is important because you can always draw general observations and insight from specifics, but you can never find the specifics if the writer gives only broad generalizations. This is the old "show, don't tell" admonition.

So, here's the assignment: Students are to go out into the school garden or a nearby park and find a comfortable place to sit. They should have a pad of paper with them. They then observe everything within a one meter radius around them and write down all they see. (This is a 45-minute exercise.) The students first think there is very little going on there—perhaps some dead grass, a single plant, etc. But the revelation is that as they keep watching, more and more of the complexity of life emerges: an ant caravan, a spider on the hunt, rotting and regenerating plants, discarded bottle caps. Students are to observe and write freely, not just sit and craft a few points or an essay. The next day, students share their observations with the class. We usually read four or five out loud and discuss them. Observations can also be typed up and posted on the wall, perhaps with some water-color sketches, if some students wish to do them.

Step 2: *Student examples.* Say to students: "These garden observations are useful in writing the interview and in discussion about observing everything that happens in an interview. Soon you will be going out and doing your own interview, and while there are three different ways to report them, the Q & A format is too often used as the lazy way out, so you want to use either the New Journalism or Studs Terkel style. Let's take a look at high school students who have done this in the past, and some of the reports they have come up with. These were done in classes taught by teachers working with the Bay Area Writing Project, which is part of the National Writing Project.

"We'll read these examples aloud in class and then decide which format the student writer is using, and how it works." (See samples: "Today Tracy, Tomorrow the World," "Nuns," "Only the Good Die Young," "An Interview with a Transsexual," and "The Religion of Revolution: Interview with Ramona Africa," pp. 27–35.)

Step 3: *Reflection.* Conduct a discussion after each reading. Note how each student took the assignment and ran with it—how they dared to go places they were afraid of, looked into future career possibilities, met people in the neighborhood about whom they had always wondered. Henry, who interviewed people in the teenage hospice clinic, actually went on to pursue a career as a psychiatric counselor in that field. Also, have students note the descriptions, the way normal settings can take on ominous overtones, as described by Tony: a group of parked cars is described as "American-made sedans" which are "guarding" the front of the "white" building.

There are a few other points students should notice about these interviews. First, many of them took the lead of Studs Terkel and went out and interviewed people who were not at the top of the heap in power and prestige. Studs Terkel would take the cop on the beat, the prostitute, the junkie, the stone mason, and draw out their dreams and their soul. He would tell their stories but always enrich our understanding of the human condition and our hopes and dreams. So remind students: Don't go interview the principal. You might know someone famous or you might be able to contact someone you wanted to get to talk to. This would make a good interview. But you might also be able to get a great interview by talking to that homeless man you see every day or the custodian in the hall.

Step 4: *Obstacles and Interview Tips.* Give students the following advice and tips:

"It is much harder to do a successful interview than you might have thought." (Look ahead to the next lesson plan—Lesson Plan No. 4, p. 14.) "The way you plan to publish the interview, or how you plan to report it, will suggest many things about how to proceed with the interview."

"Look at the problems Tony had in his interview with the Nazi (pp. 27–28). It is important that you think the interview through thoroughly ahead of time. Learn about your interview subject. Learn about his/her era. Don't interview a Pearl Harbor survivor and say, 'Well, what year did that happen?' Read up.

"Prepare at least ten questions. Write them down, since we will be sharing them in class for feedback." (You will go more deeply into the interview questions as you have students do a practice interview; see Lesson Plan No. 4, step 3. If you like, you can move that piece here, to model good question planning.)

"When you do the interview, arrive promptly. Give some thought to comportment. You are not interested in making a statement about how you look. You want to put the interviewee at ease. So think about your clothing, grooming (fingernails, hair, etc.), and language. Make sure you look and act respectful. If you are interviewing a World War II veteran, you do not want him to focus on his generational issues because of your style.

"Pretest your tape recorder. I don't know how many students have gotten to an interview and then spent 20 minutes fussing with the machine. Bring back-up batteries.

"Remember, too, that prepared questions are just a crutch. Once you get going, you should always push to follow up on what the interviewee is saying. The most important and probing questions are the follow-up questions. You are helping the person find his/her way to the heart of the story. Try to keep your questions specific and concrete, just as good writing is specific and concrete. This elicits good answers. Also, be careful not to offend the interviewee by prying into personal areas where he/she does not want to go.

"Finally, pay attention. For the duration of the interview, you must treat this person as the most fascinating, interesting, and inspiring person in the world. By paying close attention you will get the speaker to talk more, delve deeper, and think more reflectively. Also, be sure to observe the whole scene—the room, the desk, the interviewee's hands, clothes, dialect, etc. Even if you record the interview, you should also jot down very thorough notes and observations soon after you leave."

Then hand out and read together the Interview Project assignment on the next page.

PUBLISHING
Lesson Plan No. 4

OVERVIEW: Completing the interview and publishing it is a key step. Everything students have learned in the course of several weeks comes together through their own practice. As students go through this process, they begin to read *Working* and the daily newspaper with more commitment and care. There are dozens of ways this step can be elaborated on, all depending on your resources and inclinations. You may pursue interviews on one theme or one population or you may allow students random choice. But inevitably students are pleased with the final project. They review their own interview with care and carefully read the work of their peers.

Sometimes students get frustrated or even stymied during their interviews. If possible, give them a chance to regroup and find a new subject. I once had a student who tried for two weeks to get an interview with the carillon ringer at the University of California at Berkeley. She spoke to him several times on the telephone. Sometimes he seemed to

Interview Project

Take the time to prepare for your interview, to be ready to get the most out of the encounter. When the meeting or meetings with the interview subject have been completed, pay special attention to how you report the interview and how you convey the profile of this person.

1. Choose a subject (a person to interview). Report to the class on your choice and get feedback. Complete by: _____ .

2. Before the interview, have a discussion with the interviewee in which you get to know each other. Research your interviewee and the area of expertise you expect to explore. Plan at least ten questions, write them out, share them with the class. Complete by: _____ .

3. Conduct the interview. Choose a format for reporting the interview and write it up. Complete by: _____ .

be avoiding her, sometimes he set up meetings and missed them. One time she rode up the elevator and got off, only to encounter a man getting on and riding down. She didn't realize that was her bell ringer until it was too late. Even though she never got the interview, she wrote up such a fascinating account of the frustrating chase—a great piece of New Journalism—that she got an A.

The publishing aspect of this unit makes it most powerful. Classroom books are easy to create from a group of interviews. But you can also share the interviews with the subjects themselves, especially if you have had the whole class pursue interviews on a particular theme. If it is on veterans or local civil rights activists, for example, you can create a display for the lobby of the local veterans center, the local museum, or a community center. Internet and video publishing are also powerful ways of displaying such results, which can often be put on local cable public access channels.

In this way, the work of Studs Terkel comes alive, and is not a frozen cultural artifact. As students create and further the discourse and the activism of all sectors of society, as did Studs, they are also extending the writing ethic which has infused Studs's work.

Objectives for Students

- Recognize important skills needed for successful interviews.
- Coordinate and utilize all the technical aspects of the interview, including a tape recorder, camera, possibly a video camera.
- Carry out a successful interview.
- Report and publish the interview.
- Reflect on and evaluate the interview process.

TIME: Three to four days over two weeks.

MATERIALS: Material/equipment for publishing interviews, whether in booklet form, on the Internet, or even as a wall poster. On-camera documentation—still or video—is another option.

PROCEDURE:

Step 1: *Brainstorming.* After the interview assignment is given, allow students time to brainstorm, plan, plot, and worry over who to interview. It is best to have a class discussion the very next day, before some students go too far, about their plans. Go around the room and have each person describe their preliminary plans. Often this will lead to discussions about the possibilities and problems with different interview subjects. Talk to students about the technical requirements. For example, they should have a tape recorder if at all possible.

You can also require students to take a photograph of the interview subject. This makes the interview report much more powerful, no matter how you publish it. If you have digital cameras available, students who are creating a Web page can use them to load their images directly into the computer.

For some classes, video interviews can be planned. This is more complicated to set up technically, and takes more to get interviewees to relax and speak freely, but it can be a powerful way of gathering and reporting oral histories.

Step 2: *Preparation.* After students have committed to an interview and have set up the time, there is still class work to do in preparation. It is often a good idea to have the students share their ten prepared questions before the interview. Even though they are reminded that they should feel free to branch off from these ten, their core questions should be solidly planned. Students can meet in groups of three or four and read their questions to each other. Classmates should give useful feedback: Are the questions too vague and global? Do they reflect research and thought on the subject? Do they build and go somewhere? Are they honest? Students should have their questions approved by peers, and preferably by the teacher as well, before going into the interview.

To reinforce student reflection on interview techniques, you might tell them that even Terkel has no single method or technique for interviewing; he follows his own feelings. Note his discussion of his way of conducting an interview in the preface to *Division Street: America*, which he reiterates in the introduction to *Working:* "I realized quite early in this adventure that interviews, conventionally conducted, were meaningless. Conditioned clichés were certain to come. The question-and-answer technique may be of some value in determining favored detergents, toothpaste, and deodorants, but not in the discovery of men and women. There were questions, of course. But they were casual in nature—at the beginning: the kind you would ask while having a drink with someone; the kind he would ask you. The talk was idiomatic rather than academic. In short, it was conversation. In time, the sluice gates of dammed up hurts and dreams were opened."

Step 3: *Modeling.* A practice interview in front of the class is a useful exercise, especially if students show a reluctance to conduct interviews. Laury Fischer, a teacher at Diablo Valley Community College, sits on a stool in the middle of his classroom. Students are invited to ask him questions, press-conference style. They can be about life, teaching, or his biography. He answers them while a student writes the questions on a transparency.

Afterward, Fischer classifies their questions by level. Level 1 contains questions which call for a safe, objective, short answer, such as ice breakers. These are recommended for gathering background information and for making both people comfortable. Examples are: How long have you been doing this job? Where did you go to college? Did you grow up in this area?

Level 2 questions are much more interesting and are where the heart of the interview resides. These are anecdotal or evaluative. Good examples, on the subject of teaching, are: Tell me about a student you'll always remember. Tell me about a colleague you truly admire. If you were in charge of things, what would your first three items of business be? What are the most difficult parts of the job?

Level 3 consists of "X-rated" questions, and students should not ask these. They not only include taboo subjects—sex, drugs, arrests—but are also usually inappropriate—How much money do you make? Which instructors do you think are horrible? Has a student ever offered you a bribe?

Usually, all three types of questions will be asked in this "press conference" setting so you will have an opportunity to talk about each of them. But for their actual interviews, students should stick with Levels 1 and 2. Other general discussion about the questions should include making sure that they are not too vague and global. And questions that can be answered with one word are disqualified.

A student can even snap a Polaroid photo of the teacher during this practice process and put it up on the board with a quick description of the points learned in the interview. This process is not designed to create a completed interview but rather to get students to warm up and to discuss issues in interview technique. Actually, they usually jump into this activity with enthusiasm because they are curious about their teacher!

Step 4: *Discussion.* During the time actual interviews are going on, encourage students to come back with stories of their progress and to bring in problems and challenges. Review the three formats for reporting the interviews so students are very familiar with them: Q & A with a long introduction, New Journalism with the writer's personal reflection, or Studs Terkel style—first person narration with questions edited out, as seen in the examples on pages 163–166. Again, students can also be reading and discussing sections of *Working* during this period.

Step 5: *Write-up.* Transcribing the interview, editing it, and writing it up are major aspects of the interview process. Depending on the approach, students may find themselves doing extensive editing and creative writing during this phase. When students are describing the surroundings of the interview—either in the introduction of a Studs Terkel style interview or in the body of a New Journalism interview—they should keep in mind the lessons of the Garden Observation. Attention to detail, to telling gestures and movements, gives depth and body to the interview.

Step 6: *Publishing.* The student interview is an important historical record and should be shared. It's not enough to just write it up and hand it in for a grade. Students have used ingenious ways to publish what they have found. Often a class booklet of interviews is published. As mentioned earlier, you could also create a Web page to share the interviews. They could go on a poster or wall display in the classroom or in a school hallway. If the interviews were all conducted at a home for seniors or at a hospital, you could create a display for the lobby. Photographs can also be posted on a wall display, Web page, or in a booklet.

Video interviews will have to be edited, to clean up the work and put different interviews together. This can become quite time-consuming and frustrating unless you have a strong video curriculum. But you can see ways that the three reporting formats we've been discussing can be adapted to video. Michael Moore's technique is New Journalism; Bill Moyers's is Q & A, and edited profiles are often Studs Terkel's style.

One caveat: Depending on what kind of publishing you do, you may have to get permission releases. Generally, if a person has agreed to talk to the student, they are giving permission for the interview to be published. But they may think that it is only for classroom use. So if you plan something more ambitious, be sure the interviewees know what is going to happen. You don't want them surprised and angered to find their personal confessions broadcast on the Internet. This is a good reason to plan the nature of the publication of the interviews *before* students meet with their subjects, so they can answer interviewees' questions about the end result. (See sample release form, p. 45.) Some subjects choose to use a pseudonym, in which case a photograph should not be published.

Step 7: *Evaluation.* There are many ways students can evaluate this unit on interview techniques. They can write up learning logs, in which they describe what they learned and what they'd like to pursue more. They can be asked to write a short piece, in class, about the interview process and hand it in with the interview. Students can create a rubric to evaluate the interviews and give each other grades. They can also reflect on the whole project once it is published. The important thing is to get feedback for improving future lessons and to allow students to use metacognition in evaluating their learning process.

Professional Interview Model

QUESTION AND ANSWER: INTERVIEW WITH TREY PARKER AND MATT STONE, CONDUCTED BY DAVID WILD FOR *ROLLING STONE* (JULY 8, 1999).

In the following piece, David Wild writes an introduction to the interview and then records his questions and the answers from the creators of the movie and television series South Park.

It's pretty much your average animated movie musical about war, censorship, and sodomy between Saddam Hussein and Satan. But even so, in this era of teen-culture paranoia, *South Park: Bigger, Longer, and Uncut* should give this summer's edgy parents all sorts of reasons to lock up their kids. There have been rumors that Paramount, the studio releasing the movie, is scared of its subject matter. *South Park*'s creators, Matt Stone and Trey Parker, are unrepentant and justifiably proud that some of the jokes that the Motion Picture Association of America ratings board ruled too rude for the multiplex have been recycled for the *South Park* TV show.

The walls of Parker and Stone's large loftlike work space in West Los Angeles are covered with promising and profane descriptions of sequences in the film. They are willing to admit that the movie is a musical of sorts. "That will make the sixteen-year-old boys jump for joy," Stone says with a laugh. They also confess that the relationship between the bizarre but fun couple Saddam and Satan is a curiously touching love story. And, unable to contain their glee, they preview the first single from the film's soundtrack album—a wild punk-meets-*Lord of the Dance* rouser with the memorable title "What Would Brian Boitano Do?" . . .

What have you two learned about Hollywood from the process of bringing *South Park* to the big screen?

> PARKER: Well, it was a clash. We had our system for doing things, the studio had its own system. They're like, "This is how you do a movie." And we're like, "Well, this is how you make *South Park*." It was a constant battle. We were in a pretty good position of power, because our blessing—and our curse—is that we have to do everything. They can't farm it out.

So is *South Park: Bigger, Longer, and Uncut* really going to be totally uncut?

> PARKER: No, because the MPAA is in many ways way more strict than the TV people.

Are you concerned that, post-Columbine, there's a climate where our youth culture is under fire?

> PARKER: Yeah, and it's amazingly strange, because that climate is what the movie is all about, and we wrote it more than a year ago. So when [Columbine] happened, we were like, "Wow." What we wrote about in this movie came true in terms of people's attitudes. The movie is about war, and then that happened, too.

Have you ever had a moment when you felt maybe you were damaging the psyche of young America?

> PARKER: Not at all. Not for a second. We grew up with Monty Python, as fucked-up as that all was, and Dirty Harry and Charles Bronson and ultraviolence. People seem to forget that the world has been ultraviolent for a long time. Both of us—and

all our friends—grew up in that culture, and we're fine. There's nothing about Marilyn Manson that says, "Pick up a gun and kill people." And there's nothing about *South Park* that says that, either.

STONE: When anything like the Columbine thing happens, everybody—us included—is so confused and saddened. People want an explanation . . . and the explanation that some people are fucked-up—that's a scary answer, but it is the answer. When someone older does something sick, it's like, "What a psychopath, what a perverted sociopath, what a nut." When someone under the age of eighteen does something, then we have a huge problem with youth culture.

Being from Colorado, did you know that high school?

STONE: My high school, Evergreen, played against Columbine. I think it's been renovated since, but I took my SATs in its cafeteria.

Trey, when you gave the commencement speech at your high school recently, what was your opening line?

PARKER: "What the hell am I supposed to tell you people?" The speech went over great. It was different from their normal commencements. I didn't use any big words. I just talked to them pretty plainly and did a few voices. . . .

Professional Interview Model

NEW JOURNALISM: HUNTER S. THOMPSON, *HELL'S ANGELS—A STRANGE AND TERRIBLE SAGA* (NEW YORK: BALLANTINE BOOKS, 1966, PP. 133–135).

In the following excerpt, Hunter Thompson is describing a discussion he had in a small town in California named Bass Lake. Thompson is following the outlaw motorcycle club, the Hell's Angels.

I was standing in a glass phone booth in downtown Bass Lake—which consists of a small post office, a big grocery, a bar and cocktail lounge, and several other picturesque redwood establishments that look very combustible. While I was talking, Don Mohr pulled up on his bike—having breached the roadblock with his press credentials—and indicated that he was in a hurry to call the *Tribune*. My editor in Washington was telling me how and when to file, but I was not to do so until the riot was running under its own power, with significant hurt to both flesh and property . . . and then I was to send no more than an arty variation of the standard wire-service news blurb: Who, What, When, Where, and Why.

I was still on the phone when I saw a big, burr-haired lad with a pistol on his belt walk over to Mohr and tell him to get out of town. I couldn't hear much of what was going on, but I saw Mohr produce a packet of credentials, stringing them out like a card shark with a funny deck. I could see that he needed the phone, so I agreed with my man in Washington that first things would always come first, and hung up. Mohr immediately occupied the booth, leaving me to deal with the crowd that had gathered.

Luckily, my garb was too bastard for definition. I was wearing Levi's,

Wellington boots from L. L. Bean in Maine, and a Montana sheep-herder's jacket over a white tennis shirt. The burr-haired honcho asked me who I was. I gave him my card and asked why he had that big pistol on his belt. "You know why," he said. "The first one of these sonsof-bitches that gives me any lip I'm gonna shoot right in the belly. That's the only language they understand." He nodded toward Mohr in the phone booth, and there was nothing in his tone to make me think I was exempted. I could see that his pistol was a short-barreled Smith & Wesson .357 Magnum—powerful enough to blow holes in Mohr's BAAS cylinder head, if necessary—but at arm's length it hardly mattered. The gun was a killer at any range up to a hundred yards, and far beyond that in the hands of a man who worked at it. He was wearing it in a police-type holster on the belt that held up his khaki pants, high on his right hip and in an awkward position for getting at it quickly. But he was very conscious of having the gun and I knew he was capable of raising bloody hell if he started waving it around.

I asked him if he was a deputy sheriff.

"No, I'm workin' for Mr. Williams," he said, still studying my card. Then he looked up. "What are you doin' with this motorcycle crowd?"

I explained that I was only a journalist trying to do an honest day's work. He nodded, still fondling my card. I said he could keep it, which seemed to please him. He dropped it in the pocket of his khaki shirt, then tucked his thumbs in his belt and asked me what I wanted to know. The tone of the question implied that I had about sixty seconds to get the story.

I shrugged. "Oh, I don't know. I just thought I'd look around a bit, maybe write a few things."

He chuckled knowingly. "Yeah? Well, you can write that we're ready for 'em. We'll give 'em all they want."

The dusty street was so crowded with tourists that I hadn't noticed the singular nature of the group that surrounded us. They weren't tourists at all; I was standing in the midst of about a hundred vigilantes. There were five or six others wearing khaki shirts and pistols. At a glance they looked like any bunch of country boys at any rustic hamlet in the Sierras. But as I looked around I saw that many carried wooden clubs and others had hunting knives on their belts. They didn't seem mean, but they were obviously keyed up and ready to bust some heads.

The merchant Williams had hired a few private gunmen to protect his lakefront investment; the rest were volunteer toughs who'd been waiting all day for a fight with a bunch of hairy city boys who wore chains for belts and stank of human grease. I remembered the mood of the Angels up on the mountain and I expected at any moment to hear the first of the bikes coming down the hill into town. The scene had all the makings of a king-hell brawl, and except for the pistols it looked pretty even.

Just then the door of the phone booth opened behind me, and Mohr stepped out. He looked curiously at the mob, then raised his camera and took a picture of them. He did it as casually as any press photographer covering an American Legion picnic. Then he straddled his bike, kicked it to life and roared up the hill toward the roadblock.

Student Interview Model

Today Tracy, Tomorrow the World

By Tony Remy*

(An interview with the leader of the Nazi party in California)

The road soon turned very bumpy and I bounced the rest of the way until I found myself resting out in front of a white building. Half a dozen American-made sedans guarded the front and a sign which said HEADQUARTERS OF THE NATIONAL SOCIALIST WHITE PEOPLE'S PARTY kept watch over the entire neighborhood. I quietly parked my car and walked to the door. Cursing myself for not bringing some sort of weapon, I opened the door and forced my heart back down my throat and jotted down some notes. Continuing cautiously down the corridor, I noticed that my shoes were squeaking and just shook my head. "What else could happen?" I questioned myself. The hard wooden floor seemed springy to the touch of the foot and the white walls reminded me of a prison cell. I noticed a portrait hanging in the corner and decided to investigate. As I drew nearer, I recognized the fanatical face of the king rat himself, Adolf Hitler. . . .

His [the interviewee's] appearance was not that of a Gestapo Major, but that of Santa Claus. His face seemed both oldish and kindly, and his dark eyes stood out like raisins on cottage cheese. His hair was silver/gray and cut short. The wrinkles in his face made him look about sixty-five, but I couldn't be sure. The face may have surprised me, but the clothes did not. His tan shirt, with black tie and pants, carried the standard swastika on the armband. Yes, he was a Nazi all right.

---

*Most of the names listed here for interviewers and interviewees are pseudonyms.

"Now, what would you like to know?" he asked, bracing himself.

"Your name please," I responded, trying to be the confident news-man type, but failing dearly.

"I'm sorry," he said with a sigh, "but I cannot give you my name; we've been harassed much too much as it is."

"Why that dirty . . ." I thought to myself. I wanted to yell but knew my grade depended on this interview so I regained my composure.

"What are the goals of the party?" I asked, already knowing the answer.

"Our only main objective is to tear down the present government and replace it with the party's."

He had just fallen into my first trap. "Excuse me," I said smugly, "but isn't that treason?"

"My dear boy [I hated that], was it treason when the Russians, French, and Americans had their revolution? Certainly you don't con-sider Jefferson, Franklin, and Washington as traitors?"

"But wasn't that different?"

"Not as far as I'm concerned," he responded, as nonchalantly as possible.

"How do you know that there are that many people who will join you?" I asked, starting to feel more confident.

"Our nationwide membership insures this."

"About how many is that?"

"Hard to say."

"Just an estimate?" I pressed.

"How about approximately 750,000 nationwide."

"Are you serious?"

"Deadly serious," he said, sounding like a madman in a grade B movie.

"How about World War II?"

"What in particular?"

"If Nazism is so great, how did you ever lose?" Man, I hope he's not carrying a gun, I joked to myself as my pencil came to attention. . . .

Student Interview Model

Nuns

By Cindy Martin

(An interview with her sister, who has joined a convent)

Let's see, when did I decide to become a nun? Well, when I was in high school, a girlfriend and I used to joke around about becoming nuns, then suddenly it wasn't a joke anymore. My family was shocked but finally realized that I meant business. I visited a few convents and decided on Dominican Sisters. They were very helpful and urged me to go out in the world and get a job, my own apartment, and go out on dates. They don't want naïve high school girls going straight into the convent without being out in the real world first. I really learned a lot about myself and how to stand on my own two feet.

After two years, I returned to the convent and made my promises. It was a real cultural shock for me. I had to do a lot of things for the good of the community that I would have rather not done. Getting up at 5:45 A.M. is still tough for me and I'd rather not eat at the hours we have, but I'm only one out of 120 sisters who live here. It's part of the sisterhood and if it pleases God then that is all that matters. I guess there are bound to be a few unexpected inconveniences. It's like a mother with a newborn baby. She thinks it is cute and cuddly, but then she realizes she has to get up at 3:00 A.M. to feed it.

(Laughs.)

Student Interview Model

Only the Good Die Young

By Henry Paz

(A talk with terminally ill teenagers)

Two adults came in; one was a counselor, one a psychiatrist. They announced there was a guest present (namely me) and started the meeting. The discussions were altogether very depressing and especially two of them stayed in my mind. For a while, everyone talked with a young boy (age twelve) about how he started to urinate blood more than normally (as if urinating blood at all is normal, I thought). All of a sudden he started to pray and plead to God to make it stop. There was silence and then there was his crying. All of a sudden this other girl (age seventeen) who had to have more chemotherapy started to cry because she will lose all of her hair again. This will make it her fourth time. For the last part, the time was spent saying goodbye to a departing patient. He had been there for two and a half months. After hugging everyone, he began to cough; strangely, it looked like the coughing really tired him out as if he'd just run around the block. The meeting had come to an end so I went into the hall and talked for a little while before I left.

Patient (seventeen): On my sixteenth birthday, I was on an operating table, getting my uterus removed. Now they tell me it was all for nothing.

Patient (fourteen): I wish I could just die sometimes 'cause I think of my parents and all the money they're spending on me. There's no cure for what I've got. It's ridiculous.

Patient: At night I wet the bed and I wake up with blood all over me. It's been going on now for about three months. It will happen three or four times a day. It really hurts and I wish it would stop.

On the way home I cried. I couldn't help it. Now I really understood. I think I could comprehend what it would be like, how I'd react, and what life would be to me if I knew I was going to die from a terminal disease. . . .

Student Interview Model

AN INTERVIEW WITH A TRANSSEXUAL

By Rachel Leff-Kich

(Student selected subject out of curiosity about the clients her mother, a sex therapist, sees.)

Stephanie Durant is a freelance writer and artist in San Francisco. She is forty-nine. We spoke over the phone.

I'll just start by saying that I'm flattered. I think that a transsexual is probably someone that most people have never met or know anything about. They've probably seen weird images of transsexuals on television or something. I do a lot of speaking around the Bay Area to try to educate people about the realities of transsexualism. The realities and the imagery are really different.

Since I was old enough to understand anything, since I was about three, I have known that I wanted to be a girl, instead of a boy, as it was then. I had continued to know that all my life. I was born a long time ago (*laughs*) it seems to me, at a time when there was really no information about such things and you couldn't go and find it anywhere. Today, if a young person, say a teenager or in their early twenties or something, wanted to be . . . you know, felt they were transsexual, they could go to the library or they could phone a help line or, you know, there's so many resources now. In those days—I grew up in Vancouver, Canada, in the '50s—and in those days there was nothing, no information available, and if I'd sought it out, I would've probably been sent to a psychiatrist who probably would have sent me to a mental hospital.

Anyways, I know I wanted to do it, for my whole life, but I didn't know what to do about it. Also, the way society will teach you to do things, I felt very ashamed of feeling this, so I didn't really do anything about it, at least nothing major, until I was forty-two years old. I finally sort of had a nervous breakdown and thought I could not carry on. . . . My life kind of ground down to a halt and I thought I just could not carry on as a person in the world if I had to be, you know, male. I had tried and tried and I couldn't do it, so finally, at the age of forty-two, with nowhere else to turn, I finally gave in. . . .

Student Interview Model

THE RELIGION OF REVOLUTION: INTERVIEW WITH RAMONA AFRICA

By Addie Wright

(An interview with a subject the student was interested in, by telephone across the country)

Ramona Africa has been nationally respected for her constant efforts to ignite revolution. As a preacher of the MOVE religion, Ramona has a very fulfilled history of political involvement. Her speeches have influenced America's revolutionaries greatly because of the extremity of her experiences and the truth in her message.

In 1985, Ramona was the sole adult survivor of the bombing of the MOVE headquarters in Philadelphia. Six adult MOVE members were killed in the bombing, including John Africa, the organization's founder, whose actions and teachings are looked upon as legendary. Five children were also killed in this unwarranted, unjustified bombing by the Philadelphia police. After the incident, Ramona Africa lived seven years as a political prisoner in Pennsylvania. In 1996, after a trial in which she represented herself, Ramona Africa was compensated with $1.5 million by the Pennsylvania court for the 1985 destruction and murders.

The following are Ramona's words as delivered to me in answer to questions about her life, her people, and her message.

I encountered MOVE when I was twenty-four years old; I was a student at Temple University. I was about to get my bachelor's degree in political science and I was starting to get active in the things that were going on. A friend invited me to a meeting to plan a demonstration in support of

MOVE and I wanted to go. I did go. I met MOVE supporters who gave me a lot of information about things that had happened over the years that I did not even know about. I had lived in West Philadelphia where MOVE was located, all my life.

A few of my friends, well, my MOVE sisters now, told me that I did not have to take their word for what was going on and that I should come and sit in on some trials that were going on at the time. That happened to be the pretrial hearing on the August 8 murder trial. This was in 1979.

I went to court for a couple of reasons, because that was my interest, and because I intended to go to law school. So when I went to court and sat in on that trial, I was just astounded; I was flabbergasted because nothing was being conducted like I was taught it was supposed to be. I read books about the legal system, my professors talked about it, so I thought I knew how the court should work. When I sat in that room, neither the judge, the district attorney, nor the so-called defense conducted themselves like I was taught. I was shocked! I was ready to jump up and say, "You can't do that; my book says right here that you can't do that!" So that kept me coming back.

The other thing that impressed me was that MOVE people were fearlessly defending themselves; the attorneys were only back-up counselors. I had never seen people stand up and defend themselves like MOVE people. There were not intimidated by the judge, by the D.A., by the courtroom procedure, none of that. . . .

Oral History

THE FEDERAL WRITERS' PROJECT
Lesson Plan No. 1

OVERVIEW: Since Studs Terkel first began interviewing, oral history has captured the American imagination. Oral history projects engage students because they are involved in the creation of historical information, documents, and narratives perhaps otherwise unavailable. By conducting oral histories, students are not passively reading history, but rather are writing history.

On-line resources in oral history are particularly rich. This oral history unit is adapted from the on-line site which is based on the work of the Federal Writers' Project and created by the Smithsonian Institution and the Library of Congress in Washington, D.C., at http://learn ing.loc.gov/learn/lessons/oralhist/ohhome.html. The unit presents social history content and topics through the voices of ordinary people. It draws on primary sources from the Smithsonian's American Memory Collection, American Life Histories, 1936–1940.

Using these excerpts and further research in the collections, students in this lesson develop their own research questions. They then plan and conduct oral history interviews with members of their own communities.

This lesson is best taught in conjunction with a unit of study in the humanities that requires study of contemporary or recent history. For some classes, this is the Vietnam War or the Civil Rights Movement; for others, it is the local or regional economy, government studies, even a novel about recent periods of history. (For example, *Coffee Will Make You Black* by April Sinclair tells of the coming of age of an African-American girl in the '60s; *Tortilla Curtain* by T. C. Boyle is an examination of U.S.–Mexican border issues.) A great story that calls out for oral history projects is the increasing diversity of our population. From homogeneous zones and neighborhoods at midcentury, the United States is now a mixture of races and cultures, with most schools now teaching students with 10, 20, even 50 different home languages. Students will use sections of *Working* to discuss how to create a document that is a "witness to our times," then try out their own projects.

Objectives for Students

- Define "social history."
- Formulate questions about social history topics.
- Interpret changes in twentieth-century social life in the United States using existing oral histories and by conducting original interviews.

TIME: Five to six class periods, plus time to conduct oral history interviews outside of class.

MATERIALS: Computers with access to the Web; copies of *Working*.

PROCEDURE:

Step 1: *Introduction to Social History.* Ask students to brainstorm what topics are covered by the word "history." Write terms on the board, such as presidents, wars, explorers, government activities, famous people, famous inventions, family life, recreation, work, clothing, and school. Point out that different kinds of historians look at different topics within history. While many history textbooks deal with political and military history, historians also study the lives and activities of everyday people.

Step 2: Divide students into small groups. Hand out and have students read the Introduction to Social History (pp. 40–41). (Students can also read this at the Web address for Introduction to Social History: http://lcweb2.loc.gov/ammem/ndlpedu/lessons/oralhist/ohstart./html.)

Step 3: Have students discuss the importance of social history in the overall development of a historical picture of a period. Review a historical period students have studied and what kinds of additional insights can be gained from a social history profile.

Step 4: One of the key ways to develop an oral history is through interviews. Investigators, historians, and just folks go out and look at the community, observe how we live, gather data, and interview individuals. Have students read the section on the automobile in *Working*, pages 159–232. Discuss the "organizing principle" that went into this section—the view that the automobile had a tremendous effect on all aspects of American life. This is true not just for people who build them but for people who drive, regulate, and avoid them. What other aspects of modern life could be an "organizing principle" for a social history investigation, something that could be investigated through research and interviews? Some likely candidates: the impact of the computer, immigration and diversity, the Gulf War (or other global conflicts).

Step 5: Studs Terkel was inspired to do his interviews in part by his work in the Federal Writers' Project. Participants gathered some of the most important oral history documentation of the United States in the 1930s—documentation that has gone into a social history of that period which is still important to this day. Have students look at this record of the 1930s as maintained by the Smithsonian Institution in Washington, D.C. Start with a reading on the importance of oral history in the creation of social history. Have students read the handout Oral History and the Federal Writers' Project (pp. 42–44), in groups.

Step 6: Have students analyze some oral histories collected by the Federal Writers' Project. Each group chooses one interviewee [informant] for the Federal Writers' Project to read and discuss. Hand out source sheet (p. 45).

Step 7: Have student groups make presentations on the person from the 1930s they have chosen to study. They will use the interview information gathered by the Federal Writers' Project for these reports. Besides oral presentations, they can create visual support to accompany the board, written papers, or radio shows.

They should be able to explain to the class:

- What the person does for a living.
- What personal concerns and interests the person has.

- What one learns about America in the '30s from the person's personal life.
- What new dimensions can be added to American history as a result of this interview.

Step 8: *Evaluation.* The class should complete this lesson plan with an evaluation. This can be a class discussion or a written learning log.

COLLECTING ORAL HISTORY
Lesson Plan No. 2

OVERVIEW: This lesson plan allows classes to conduct oral history projects that contribute to local social histories. It is also important to preserve the gathered data in its raw form as well as in its presentation format, for these investigations represent legitimate social history that will indeed be examined and evaluated by future historians. Many of the steps used to conduct these interviews are developed more fully in the Interview Unit of this book. The development steps represented in this unit focus on the ways the interviews are used as part of a social history investigation.

Objectives for Students

- Use oral history interview techniques to gather information about social history.
- Analyze, interpret, and conduct research using oral histories.

TIME: Four or five days of class time plus interviewing time (10–14 days).

Introduction to Social History

DEFINING SOCIAL HISTORY People often think the study of history means studying governments, battles, and national leaders. These are important history topics, but historians learn much about history by studying the lives of everyday people as well.

Social history is the history of the everyday experiences and beliefs of ordinary people. Social historians look at teachers, store clerks, factory workers, police officers, the unemployed, children, computer programmers—all kinds of people you might meet in your own life.

The number of social history topics is huge because social history looks at every aspect of day-to-day life—family life, recreation, work, social life, religious beliefs, and more. Most social historians study one group of people (such as Japanese Americans), one particular area (such as the Great Plains in Nebraska), or a specific topic within social history (such as family life).

ASKING SOCIAL HISTORY QUESTIONS Imagine that you are a social historian studying family life in Massachusetts in three different periods of history. What kinds of questions would you ask?

Here are examples of questions you might research:

- What kind of food does this family usually eat? How do they get their food?

- What kinds of natural resources are available where this family lives? How do these resources influence the types of food, shelter, and clothing available?

- Does every child in the family attend school? Why or why not?

- Can every member of the family read and write? Why or why not? What kinds of books are available to the family?

- How important is religion to the family's life?

- What work does each member of the family do?

- Does the family own property? Why or why not?

- Which family members can vote? Which family members do vote?

- What transportation does the family use to get around?

- What games do children play? What do adults do for relaxation?

- What family activities might be considered an art or craft today?

SOURCES FOR LEARNING ABOUT SOCIAL HISTORY

Social historians use many sources—diaries, letters, songs, census information, artifacts including clothing and tools, photographs, public records including birth, marriage, and death certificates, and oral histories.

In this lesson, you will use oral histories to explore social history. You will start by studying oral histories collected as part of the Federal Writers' Project in the 1930s. Then you will conduct some oral history interviews yourself.

This handout can also be found on the Library of Congress Learning Page: http://lcweb2.loc.gov/ammem/ndlpedu/lessons/oralhist/ohstart.html.

Oral History and the Federal Writers' Project

WHAT IS ORAL HISTORY? Recording oral history is a way to gather information from people who took part in past events. Gathering oral histories is the technique of interviewing people who lived through historic events or time periods and recording their answers. The person being interviewed is often called the interview subject.

THE FEDERAL WRITERS' PROJECT During the Depression of the 1930s, the U.S. government created programs to employ out-of-work Americans. One such program, designed to provide work for unemployed writers, was called the Federal Writers' Project. This project employed more than 300 writers. These writers collected stories (oral histories) from more than 10,000 people across America from 1935 through 1942.

Many people who became famous writers were interviewers for the Federal Writers' Project. They included Zora Neale Hurston, John Cheever, Ralph Ellison, Saul Bellow, Richard Wright, and May Swenson. Their experiences talking to ordinary Americans helped shape their later writing.

About 3,000 oral histories recorded by the Federal Writers' Project are now available on-line through the Smithsonian's American Memory Collection, American Life Histories, 1936–1940. You will be using these life histories in this lesson.

HOW FEDERAL WRITERS COLLECTED LIFE HISTORIES Federal writers conducted their oral history interviews before tape recorders were readily available. The writers took extensive notes, then wrote up results of their interviews using their notes and their memories. Some writers reported that the more notes they took, the more people were willing to talk. When the people being interviewed saw someone write down their words, they began to feel their stories were important.

The director of the Federal Writers' Project, Benjamin Botkin, asked the writers to listen for speech patterns and vocabulary that were unique to an area or an ethnic group. The famous writer Ralph Ellison said that his experience listening to speech patterns during the Federal Writers' Project helped him accurately represent the sound of black speech in his masterpiece novel, *Invisible Man*.

Botkin also wanted the writers to make interview subjects "feel important. Well-conducted interviews serve as social occasions to which informants come to look forward." (The interview subjects were called informants by the project.) Different writers used different ways to make people comfortable. For example, Ralph Ellison said, "I would tell some stories to get people going and then I'd sit back and try to get it [their stories] down as accurately as I could."

WHAT INFORMATION DID THE WRITERS GATHER? The writers filled out forms as part of their interviews. The forms asked for the following information about the people being interviewed:

Ancestry

Place and date of birth

Family

Place lived in

Education

Occupations and accomplishments

Special skills and interests

Community and religious activities

Description of informant

Beyond the information requested on the form, writers could ask interview subjects about any aspect of their lives. (Used by permission from the Library of Congress, http://lcweb2.loc.gov/ammem/ndlpedu/lessons/oralhist/ohfwp.html.)

ANALYZING ORAL HISTORIES You can find complete versions of the oral histories collected by the Federal Writers' Project, and many more interviews, in the on-line American Memory Collection at http://lcweb2.loc.gov/ammem/wpaintro/wpahome.html, American Life Histories, 1936–1940.

In your group, choose one of the primary source sets shown below. Read as many excerpts on-line as your teacher assigns. In your group discuss and record answers to the questions that accompany each interview.

When you have finished answering the questions, as a group select a research topic that you want to investigate further that is related to your primary source set. Your group might want to investigate a different aspect of the topic during the same time period, or investigate the same topic in another time period.

Once your group has chosen a topic for further research, go ahead, on the Web site, to Background Research for Oral History Interviews, found at the Library of Congress Web site, http://lcweb2.loc.gov/ammem/ndlpedu/lessons/oralhist/ohstart.html.

You can order written and taped copies of these interviews on the Web at: http://lcweb2.loc.gov/ammem/wpaintro/wpahome.html.

PRIMARY SOURCES

WORKING WOMEN IN THE 1930s

I Ain't No Midwife (1939)

Packinghouse Workers (1939)

Italian Feed (1940)

Miss Henrietta C. Dozier (1939)

DANCING AS A FORM OF RECREATION, 1890s–1930s

Charles Cole (1939)

Mrs. Charley Huyck (1939)

Old Time Dance Calls (1938)

AMERICANS AND THE AUTOMOBILE

Roy A. Morse (1938)

Yankee Innkeeper (undated)

Dunnell #13 (1939)

Transportation (1939)

This handout can also be found on the Library of Congress Learning Page http://lcweb2.loc.gov/ammem/ndlpedu/lessons/oralhist/ohdir.html.

MATERIALS: Materials needed for interviews (tape recorder, camera, etc.) and for publishing, depending on how students plan to create a final presentation.

PROCEDURE:

Step 1: Have students choose a topic of social history to research in their community. This can be local economic history, a major community institution (the museum, a factory, the port, etc.), the impact of a historic event on the community (for example, they can study the Vietnam War by talking to veterans, or by talking to those who were in the community at the time), a social issue of the day (immigration and diversity, local gay history, etc.) or even an "organizing principle," such as the impact of the computer. Another powerful research project is to look for more subtle and less dramatic stories, themes of research that shine a light on the daily life of people in the community; for example, children's toys and play, family recreation, teenage social life, etc.

You may have the whole class function as a research group or break it into teams of four or five, each of which will pursue one area. Again, if you use teams or group work, you can have each team do a different aspect of the same issue (for example, one group interviews Vietnam veterans, one interviews widows, one interviews draft resisters and activists, one interviews parents and children, etc.).

Step 2: Have students conduct background research on their chosen topics. This means students should study the available historical sources, review local documents, and conduct on-line research. They should, as much as possible, become expert in the area they plan to focus on. This initial research should be shared with the class and discussed. Ask: What further information do we need to develop to create a strong social history on the subject?

Step 3: Each group, or the whole class, meets now to write down three research questions they will try to answer by conducting oral history interviews. These questions will serve as the starting point for planning the interviews. Students can use the lessons learned in the Interview Unit in this process. The difference will be that a number of interviews are to be conducted and these will all have the goal of answering the three research questions the group has agreed upon.

Step 4: Review the three research questions each group wants to answer. Then, have the group write down at least ten interview questions to help gather information about the research topic they are studying. They should think of things people can tell them about their first-hand experiences with the research topic. Questions should require more than a yes or no answer. When the list of questions is complete, have students role play with the questions: Are the questions clear and easy to understand? Will the questions you have devised give you the answers you are looking for?

Step 5: Students should have about two weeks to complete their interviews. Sometimes there are problems setting them up; other times second meetings are required. Often the most difficult job is finding a person to interview. Students need to be doing outreach, networking, and getting references from one contact for another. When they have settled on a person to interview, they'll need to have him or her fill out a release form (see below). Remind them to consider also getting photographs of the interview subject to illustrate a report booklet or class presentation.

Step 6: Sample Release Form. Students should check with the school office for the school's guidelines on release forms. It might be best for students to create their own forms. The following is a sample release form that can be adapted.

Sample Release Form

In view of the historical value of this oral history interview, I (name of interview subject) knowingly and voluntarily permit (name of student interviewer, name of class, and name of school) the full use of this information for educational purposes.

Signature (signature of interview subject)
Date (date of interview)

Step 7: When students have completed their interviews, ask: Did the oral history interview help answer their prepared questions? Make sure they preserve everything from the interview: the raw notes, any tapes made, and photographs. These will be used to create a final report, but should also be turned in and preserved for future historians.

Have students write tentative summaries of their research results and decide how their group will present these findings to the class.

Step 8: *Group presentations.* On the due date for group presentations, allow time for each group to describe its interview and research results. The group presentation should be brief and inform the class about the interview results and what was discovered about the research topic. Students can also create a formal report that can be published on the Web or made into a booklet.

Then conduct a general class discussion to summarize the experience of the interviews and what students learned about their social history research topics. The following questions may be useful:

- What was the most surprising piece of information your interviews generated? Why was it surprising?
- What types of interview questions led to relevant, interesting answers? What types of interview questions were less effective?
- Was it hard to keep interview subjects on the topic? What strategies worked to pull your subject back to the focus of the interview?
- What good follow-up questions did you ask?
- What might have made the interview more productive?
- Did you ever question the accuracy of the information the interview subject provided? Why or why not?
- What other sources might you check to see if the interview subject provided accurate information?
- Based on your interviews and those you read in the American Life Histories Collection, what changes have occurred in the lives of everyday Americans over the last 100 years? How significant do you think these changes are?
- Through the interviews, what information did you gather about causes of change in everyday life? For example, were changes in work related to changes in technology? To society's ideas about the role of women?

Step 8: *Evaluation.* Students can evaluate the social history project in many ways. Start with the class discussion. You can then ask each student to write a one-page essay on one of the following topics:

- What was the most significant change in the lives of every-day Americans identified by your research?
- What evidence did you find of this change? What other sources might you consult to confirm the significance of this change?
- Why do you think oral history is a useful tool for understanding the past? What are oral history's strengths? What are its limitations?

Students can also work in their groups to create museum displays on their social history topics. Displays should:

- Illustrate significant changes in the lives of everyday Americans identified by the group's research;
- Provide evidence in support of those changes (such as excerpts from class interviews and the American Life Histories Collection, artifacts, and information from other sources).

Students can host an open house for their interviewees at which they present their displays. They can also participate in Local Legacies, a program to ". . . highlight, document, and preserve the richness of America's heritage. . . ." The Local Legacies program is part of the Library of Congress's Gifts to the Nation in celebration of its Bicentennial in 2000. One example is the Montana Heritage Project, which fosters projects in local schools teaching students how to research and document local cultural heritage. You can contact the Local Legacies program through the Library of Congress Web site at http://learning.loc.gov/learn/lessons/oralhist/ohhome.html.

Issues in Biography

READING BIOGRAPHY
Lesson Plan No. 1

OVERVIEW: It is often said that oral history is a rough draft of history, and an interview is a rough draft of biography. After completing the Interview Unit, students should be more aware of the role of authorship in shaping the way a person's story is told, represented, and understood. This is a short unit to help students consider the controversies and issues that exist in the writing of biography and history.

Here students will use *Working* to consider issues in biography and in historical evidence. Oral history is just a current and popular form of such evidence gathering. It is possible to form a bridge from the problems of finding the truth in oral history to broader historical questions. In this unit, students get to grapple, in an accessible way, with issues of importance at the highest levels of scholarship.

Like Studs Terkel's work, biography is not constructed to inform about just one life. The interest (and value) in reading biography arises from the fact that any individual life has threads that tie it to the larger cultural and historical world. Look at the incredible insights that Piaget gained into child psychology by simply observing his own children. People are not independent but rather are a part of the human family. As Yeats said, "There is nothing but a stream of souls, that all knowledge is biography."

Students learn in this lesson to be skeptical readers but also more active ones. They can be hooked by personal stories and use them to dig into important issues in scholarship.

The method I am proposing for biography is related to the methods of Sherlock Holmes and also to those of Sigmund Freud. If one approaches an archive with the right questions, one carries a series of important keys to locked doors. The right doors will open if the right questions are asked; the mountains of trivia will melt away, and essences will emerge.

—From "The Figure Under the Carpet" by Leon Edel,
in *Telling Lives: The Biographer's Art*,
edited by Marc Pachter, p. 24.

Objectives for Students

- Understand issues of perspective, thesis, and evidence in biography.
- Recognize the connections between the fields of history, anthropology, and literature.
- Develop and demonstrate skills of analysis and evaluation in examining text.
- Strengthen group discourse practice in critical thinking.

TIME: One to two weeks.

MATERIALS: Copies of *Working;* one set of tapes of *Remembering Slavery*, edited by Ira Berlin, Marc Favreau, and Steven Miller; other examples of biography; class sets of biographies.

PROCEDURE:

Step 1: Have the class read the Introduction to *Working.* For Terkel, a series of interviews constitutes historical evidence, collected information about an era, a group of people, a place. Ask students: What does his book say about the American work experience in the middle of the century—in other words, what is his thesis? (He avoids directly stating this thesis in the body of the work, but his introduction suggests some points he wants to get across.) What is Terkel's method of gathering evidence to support his thesis? Do you think he was open-ended about his thesis (that he did not draw conclusions until he finished his field work) or did he start out and stick with a set thesis? What do you think is the best method for such investigations?

Wayne Urban (see *Writing Educational Biography,* edited by C. Kridel, p. 103) talks about problems he encountered when trying to fit national research he had done on teacher unions into a thesis he had developed when studying unions in Atlanta: ". . . In pursuit of establishing and pursuing a thesis, I tended to shape and pick and choose that evidence regarding the non-Atlanta organizations which supported the argument I had developed in my case study." He found the problem in his work to be the pressure to "look for the overarching thesis that will encompass all of the myriad shards of reality. This search for generalization I attributed in particular to those historians who stress the social scientific aspect of their work. They want to study reality in ways akin to the practice of those social scientists who value generalization and prediction over particularity and idiosyncrasy."

In some ways, oral history and biography are both about the individual life, as well as about the perception of the individual biographer. So perhaps it frees us from the pressure to fit reality into a particular thesis. Nevertheless, even in these fields, points of view and positions, either conscious or subconscious, become evident. By the end of this unit, students should discover what anthropologists know: that it is crucial to approach research or interviews with a point of view or thesis. If you go out there like an empty cipher, you will come back only with a series of tapes. However, if you must enter the project with a thesis, you must also be willing to change your thesis as evidence piles up. Those two steps—starting with a thesis or point of view, and adjusting the thesis based on research and experience—are the key to writing biography. The biographer is responsible to the truth, but also to telling an interesting and compelling story. This is why Desmond McCarthy calls biographers "artists in oath."

Step 2: *Example 1.* Print and distribute the excerpt that follows from the Ken Kann book *Comrades and Chicken Ranchers: The Story of a California Jewish Community* (Cornell University Press, 1993). Kann grapples with the issues in evidence gathering and thesis formation. Discuss how his approach is similar to or different from Terkel's.

EXCERPT FROM KENNETH KANN'S *COMRADES AND CHICKEN RANCHERS: THE STORY OF A CALIFORNIA JEWISH COMMUNITY*

Over the course of eight years, I conducted some two hundred tape-recorded interviews with members of the Petaluma Jewish community and a few gentile observers. I accumulated an enormous mass of spoken words, all of which I transcribed verbatim. Those transcribed interviews are the basis for the story that follows.

From the beginning of the work on this book, I decided to tell the community's history entirely in the words of the people I interviewed. Like many other oral historians, I was enchanted by the people I interviewed and intoxicated by the stories they told me. I quickly decided that I would not tell their story as an omniscient historical narrator or participant-observer sociologist; rather, the Petaluma Jewish chicken ranchers should tell their own community history through their own recollections in their own language. I thought that they could best evoke the experiences of a pogrom, of a chicken-house flood, of a community political clash, or of one generation's attempt to understand another. I believed that they could best reveal their shrewdness and their blindness about their own personal experience, their insights, and myths about their own history.

At the same time, I wanted to highlight certain historical and sociological patterns I saw in the lives of the community's individuals and families and groups and generations. I sought to avoid the great trap of oral history, wherein historians become so seduced by narrators and interviews that they merely provide an anthology of verbatim conversations without conveying any larger meaning to the reader. I regarded the Petaluma Jewish community as more than a collection of fascinating people who told good stories. In this unique little Jewish chicken-ranching community, I saw a microcosm of the great patterns of immigration and assimilation, ethnic community life, and ethnic identity in twentieth-century America. I wanted to convey that epic tale through the color and passion of the Petaluma Jewish experience. I could not do it simply by transcribing interviews.

I thereby encountered the central problem of oral history: How does the oral historian give perspective to someone else's experience without violating that person's view of his or her own experience? How does the oral historian provide historical and sociological perspective on the personal experience of narrators, particularly where the narrators are unaware of those perspectives or disagree with those perspectives? Resolving this methodological and ethical problem became fundamental to my construction of this book.

To turn these spoken narratives of the Petaluma Jews into a written narrative, I selected and arranged their words so as to convey my own perspectives on their community history. I chose which narrators to include and which to exclude, which interviews to emphasize and which to ignore, which interview passages to use and which to omit. Beyond that, I have placed one narrator's story alongside another's for contrast, for agreement, for illumination of truths and lies and insights and myths—for any number of reasons that were mine rather than theirs. These decisions and selections are typical of all historical writing insofar as the historian must always decide which sources to rely on in support of his or her themes and interpretations. Other historians employing the same source materials could make countless other decisions about selection and placement, depending on their own perspectives. In this case they are able and welcome to do so, because all my source materials are being deposited with the research library of the Judah L. Magnes Museum in Berkeley, California.

Kenneth Kann, *Comrades and Chicken Ranchers: The Story of a California Jewish Community* (Ithaca, N.Y.: Cornell University Press, 1993).

Step 3: *Example 2.* Find and discuss with students other examples of the authorial voice in oral history and biographical evidence. One controversy that would make an interesting discussion topic concerns the *Shoah* project. This is the collection of oral testimony on the Holocaust sponsored by film director Steven Spielberg. The project involves gathering the stories of Holocaust survivors and keeping them on videotape for an archive of collective memory and for future study. This is a monumental and crucial task because of the sheer volume of stories. As a collective autobiography, this project will live on forever as one of the main pieces of evidence on the Holocaust, a resource that students of all ages—our future historians—will visit again and again. This effort is important, especially as survivors are dying every year.

Some, however, have criticized the way these testimonials are "framed"—that is, the way they are set up and recorded. The issue of archival truth becomes important, as such a massive collection may one day come to stand for history. Consider how modern anthropologists have raised many criticisms of Theodore Kroeber's work with Ishi, in *Ishi, the Last of His Tribe* (1961). Kroeber went a long way toward explaining and preserving the tale of some near-extinct indigenous people of California. But in doing so, he actually had Ishi live in a museum and allowed the public to come and view him as a curiosity; he constructed a version of Ishi's life that was partly true and partly a projection of his own desires and interests. Kroeber took only the information that he needed without considering how best to preserve Ishi's life and culture.

For similar reasons, some historians are concerned about the *Shoah* project and the way the stories are prodded and developed. Each subject is videotaped with professional-quality technical support and time frames. Each interview is neat, clean, clear, and 45 minutes long. And, perhaps so as not to depress the viewers too much, each story appears to have some uplift at the end, some redeeming moment, some positive glimmer of hope. But in some ways, the Holocaust is such a terrible episode in history that it points to unspeakable realities that would seem to preclude any positive result. Thus, is *Shoah* a true picture of the Holocaust, or is it the view of the recorders? Some have said of Spielberg's work that it is "Disney meets the Holocaust." Discuss this idea with the students. Is that judgment too harsh? How would they go about making sure that the historical evidence was untarnished by bias?

Step 4: *Example 3.* Often, the social class of the interviewers will influence the kind of story that is told. One of the most compelling collections of oral history is a 1930s series of tapes called *Remembering Slavery*. It a collection made by the Works Progress Administration (WPA) during the Depression in the 1930s and remastered by Ira Berlin. It is the oral testimony of ex-slaves, people who remember the time of slavery. As collective autobiographies, they are compelling and quite amazing.

Students can also read other slave narratives, many of which were written in the nineteenth century. Author Toni Morrison has pointed out that these narratives were written with a single purpose, to say: "I was here, this is what happened, and I want to change things."

Also worth exploring is Alexis de Tocqueville's *Democracy in America* (1835, 1840). As a French liberal democrat, de Tocqueville was thrilled by the evidence of democracy in the United States. But he paid scant attention to the slaves who would later write and speak narratives about their trials. Discuss with students what kind of story is told about the African-American experience by a white democrat? By African Americans themselves? How can a truthful or at least legitimate story be told across the great racial divide in America?

For those who are interested, check out examples of cross-race history and study, such as *In Red and Black: Marxian Explorations in Southern and Afro-American History* (1968) by Eugene Genovese; *The Ways of White Folks* (1934) by Langston Hughes; and "Black Subject, White Biographer" by Wayne Urban in *Writing Educational Biography* (1999), edited by Craig Kridel.

Find and share other short biographies, "biographical sketches," that students can easily evaluate and use as models for their own writing in the next lesson.

Step 5. *Historical background on biography and autobiography.* The following can be given as a handout or mini-lecture:

The art of writing biography goes through various phases and fashions.

While early historians like Herodotus in the fifth century BCE relied on interviews and testimony, some of which were reported verbatim, perhaps the first Western biographer was Plutarch, the Greek biographer and moralist who wrote in his *Life of Alexander*, "It must be borne in mind that my purpose is not to write histories but lives. . . . Sometimes

. . . an expression or a jest informs us better of their characteristics and inclinations, than the most famous sieges, the greatest armaments, or the bloodiest battles whatsoever."

Plutarch looked for broad methods to develop evidence, but he was still interested in the lives of great men—those who had the greatest impact on history. During the Middle Ages, biographies set up moral and religious role models. The lives of saints were told as exemplary life stories. Really, up to the seventeenth century, biography was hagiography—the elevation and honoring of great men.

With the coming of the Renaissance and the development of secular culture and publishing, biography changed dramatically. James Boswell's *Life of Samuel Johnson, LL.D.* (mid-eighteenth century), was based on decades of personal observation, giving the transcribed narrative the force of literature. James Boswell emphasized the importance of evidence: "We cannot look into the hearts of men, but their actions are open to observation."

After Sigmund Freud, biographers used psychological insights to probe the characters of their subjects, often—in the post-Victorian era—enjoying bringing down the self-important. Perhaps the most famous version of this type of biography, the one that debunks the heroic figures of the past, is Lytton Strachey's *Eminent Victorians* (1918), which pinned the motivation for various actions on subconscious and psychological drives. Strachey's contribution was to humanize and open his subject up to a thorough examination, as opposed to the panegyrics of the past.

It is important to put this story of biography, which follows Western cultural history, into the context of world culture. Other cultures have their own ways of remembering, of allowing the values and the spirit—the voice—to be carried on. Alex Haley made many of us aware of the powerful griot traditions of African peoples—of the oral historian who carried on family stories and memories. Family histories, complete with specific testimony, go back thousands of years in China. And indigenous peoples of the Americas have always remembered and repeated testimony from the past.

Narrative approaches in biography are generally divided into: (1) scholarly chronicle (which is a recitation of facts), (2) critical study (the author's analysis of the subject, and (3) literary—pure—biography (which is a story in narrative form).

Today biography has exploded in many directions. There are stories of the common folk as well as of the famous. Oral histories collected by the WPA have, since World War II, evolved to include whole biographies of common folk. One of the great biographies of the twentieth century is *All God's Children* by Theodore Rosengarten. This story of Ned Cobb, a black Southern sharecropper, is itself an "oral biography," a story of his life based on a series of in-depth interviews.

We have also seen the development of the collective biography, a portrait of a group of people. Then there are authors who use biography to deconstruct historical periods, while others seek to imagine alternate scenarios. Working-class people are now subjects of biography. People of color and women, whose contributions historically have gone unacknowledged, are now the subject of biography. Gay narratives previously secret—such as the gay side of the life of civil rights activist Bayard Rustin as explored in Brian Freeman's *Civil Sex*—are now examined.

The picture is not all one of confusion and chaos, however. It is simply that we live in an age of abundant information, exploding both in publishing technology and in expression. Now, more than ever, students need to acquire critical capacities, the ability to read, analyze, and critique various versions of a story. We no longer demand that the student find the "objective" truth in a story. It is enough to apprehend the various truths, and to have the critical capacity to understand where different versions are coming from.

Step 6: *Site visit.* Most cities and many towns have museums or sections of museums devoted to a profile of someone famous. There is the Henry Ford Museum near Detroit, the Mark Twain exhibit at the Blackhawk Museum in Danville, California, the Biographical Imaginings presentation at the University of South Carolina's Museum of Education, the Frederick Douglass home in Washington D.C., and hundreds more.

Make a class trip to visit such a location. Have the students examine the kind of evidence that is included there. What thesis or point of view did the curator have in creating the display? What are some strengths and weaknesses of the display?

Step 7: *Discussing autobiography.* Such an examination would not be complete without considering some examples of autobiography. The genres of memoir and autobiography have expanded tremendously in the past decades. It is possible to trace the form from Caesar's self-promoting

Commentaries (44 BCE) and St. Augustine's *Confessions* (397) to Jean-Jacques Rousseau's *Confessions* (1770). While taking the stance of admitting error, these authors mostly explained and glorified themselves. Perhaps the most famous autobiography as religious polemic is *Apologia Pro Vita Sua* by Cardinal John Henry Newman (1864).

Where there is controversy in biography, there is more in autobiography. No sooner does someone tell their story than someone is explaining how it could not have been that way. There has been controversy over political autobiography from the time of Ben Franklin to Robert Reich's recent *Locked in the Cabinet*. (See the *New York Times*, June 15, 1997, p. E5.) *The Autobiography of Malcolm X* has been viewed differently over the years. When first released in 1964, it was considered to contain his own words, recorded with some help by Alex Haley. More recently it has been described as authored by Haley with the help of Malcolm X. The accuracy of the detail in the book has also been questioned, but this is considered less important than the overall impact. A similar controversy is swirling over the autobiography of a Guatemalan peasant, Rigoberta Menchu. She won the Nobel Prize for her story, but some of the details have since been questioned.

Sometimes people pretend to write an autobiography when it is not actually that. One famous case is *The Autobiography of Alice B. Toklas* by Gertrude Stein (1933), which poses as a piece by Stein's secretary-friend Toklas. Toklas wrote her own autobiography 30 years later, in *What Is Remembered* (1963). A recent controversy has arisen over the decision of the archivist of the Martin Luther King, Jr., papers, Clayborne Carson, to manufacture a work he entitled *The Autobiography of Martin Luther King, Jr.*, mixing speeches and papers with his own invented first-person narrative.

Memoirs are often written to clarify a historical point or to explain a psychological or personal experience that can be generalized. A recent mode of memoir writing—the confession of failings and abuse—has come into favor along with certain narrative approaches.

Step 8: *Reflection.* Students can reflect on this material in a number of ways. They can set up a debate about a certain biographical work; they can have a roundtable discussion about a museum display; they can write a journal on issues in oral history and biography.

Step 9: *Critical reading.* For a final activity, students should read a complete biography. This can be either a class reading of the same book or each student reading a book of his/her choice. Or, you can set up "book circles" with groups of five students each. Each group forms a reading circle focusing on one title. Students can create a group journal (a different person writes in it each night), structured discussions, and reports for the class. For more background on this process and a framework for teaching it, see *Literature Circles* by Harvey Daniels (New York: Stenhouse, 1994).

Regardless of how you structure the class for this project, students can write a paper that explains the main thesis of the author, deduces the point of view of the writer, summarizes the main points learned about the subject, and evaluates the effectiveness of the biography. Some of the points you may want the student to cover in the paper include: Did the author tell a good story—and what are the elements that make a good story? Did he/she dramatize without falsifying? What was his/her narrative approach? Did the author stick to a public story or enter the subject's private life? Is it more political or artistic or philosophical or psychological in its approach? Does the author have a social goal in the biography—that is, does he/she elevate someone of previously low status, criticize the status quo, support the status quo? What changes in society does the author suggest would be beneficial?

Such papers can be shared in a read-around and discussion as a way for the class to reinforce and extend the insights gained in the unit.

WRITING BIOGRAPHY
Lesson Plan No. 2

OVERVIEW: As students try their own hand at biography and auto-biography, they recognize more clearly that important choices must be made in deciding what to include. They see first-hand that it is important to approach the work with a plan or structure—a thesis—but to also be willing to modify that plan as they learn more. They should consider:

- When is this bias and when is this an appropriate point of view? We cannot fall into extreme relativism, claiming that everything is in the eye of the beholder, but we can no longer be seduced by the illusion that only one objective, factual story exists.
- What kind of narrative approach will they adopt? How will they turn the jumble of information into a compelling story? Can they then circle back and check that they are true to the subject? This is being what Desmond McCarthy calls "artists in oath."
- How do they decide where to place the boundaries of the narrative? What information is appropriate to make public and where does the subject retain his/her right to privacy?
- Do the students feel they really got to know their biographical subject or is their story just a projection? What were the barriers to getting to know him/her well? How do their own biographies impact their ability to interpret the subject?
- What does the biography reveal about status and power? Has the student chosen to tell the story of the unpraised? Or have they brought a new perspective to someone who was well known?

Objectives for Students

- Recognize the issues in biography and historical evidence.
- Practice creating a narrative/story that is compelling and sticks to the truth.
- Work with peers to develop and critique a writing plan.
- Evaluate one's own work in writing biography and in creating a memoir.

TIME: This process can be spread over two to four weeks.

MATERIALS: Model biographical sketches and memoirs; material for publishing, whether as a class booklet, a wall display, or a Web page.

PROCEDURE:

Step 1: *Review.* Discuss with the class the main points of Biography Lesson Plan No. 1.

Step 2: *Interviews.* Discuss the interviews students have done. (Look back to the interview process. If you have not done this unit, just conduct a modified version of the unit and have students do one interview with someone in the community.) Ask: What would it take to turn this interview into a biography? What decisions did you make in structuring this report, in asking questions, and in the way you edited it?

Step 3: *Biography assignment.* Next, have students turn the interview into a biography. It won't really be a book but it will be a "biographical sketch" of five to ten pages. Remind students that biography cannot be created from a single interview. They must seek more perspectives. Have them conduct two more interviews with people who know the subject, and use five sources of information that are not interviews: documents (papers or letters written by the subject, papers *about* him/her), report cards, artifacts, or awards.

Step 4: *Group meeting.* Have students sit in groups of three. Have each student in turn present his/her biography subject, the interview, and the other evidence that has been gathered. Have groups discuss the main point, or thesis, that will be developed about the subject. They should decide what kind of approach to take to the subject—political, psychological, etc.

Other important points for students to discuss in planning to write their biographical sketch are:

- What issues are private and should not be aired and what is or should be public?
- What is the core story that will keep the reader interested?
- What are the issues of status and power: are they working to dignify someone who has been unrecognized, to praise someone well known, to break a myth?

- What limitations does their own story, their own status, their own perspective create in trying to write a biography?

As students meet with their groups, especially as they are working through their biographical sketch, they will encounter problems. I find that it is not helpful to define the types of problems they will have ahead of time, simply because it adds up to too much information for students to absorb at a time when they do not see its importance. But as they struggle with the project, you can begin to categorize the main issues biographers grapple with.

There are basically two main types of research problems in biography. The first is the problem of **documentation**. They will find gaps in information, problems of access to something they need to know, and ethical problems of how to get or report information. The second problem is one of **interpretation**: how do they ascribe motives to the person? Are they being accurate? Is their fascination with the subject blinding them to a clear assessment?

Allow about a week for students to finish the biographical sketch.

> The other half is his real battle, the most difficult part of his task—his search for what I call the figure under the carpet, the evidence in the reverse of the tapestry, the life-myth of a mask. In an archive, we wade simply and securely through paper and photocopies and related concrete materials. But in our quest for the life-myth, we tread on dangerous speculative and inferential ground, ground that requires all of our attention, all of our accumulated resources.
>
> —From "The Figure Under the Carpet," by Leon Edel, *Telling Lives: The Biographer's Art*, edited by Marc Pachter, p. 24.

Step 5: *Critique.* Have students bring in their biographical sketches for a group critique. Depending on the situation, you may give them the option of having the subject of the biography read the sketch to the class. Then the class can interview him/her to get feedback. The student may have a good biography and get negative feedback from the subject, since often people recoil at any attempts to represent them. A caveat here: This process might result in much self-censorship by the students. So you should consider whether this step will help or hurt. Do not share biographies if they will upset or anger the subject.

> Curiosity about the private life of a public man may be of
> three kinds: the useful, the harmless, and the impertinent.
>
> —T. S. Eliot

Step 6: *Reflecting on the past.* An alternative approach to biography writing is for students to attempt a biographical sketch on a person long dead. This is more of a research paper but incorporates biographical narrative approach. The danger with using famous people is that you often will get simply an encyclopedia report. Try to find a subject for the biography who is not so famous, and who does not have a reputation.

Here's another way to do it: Have students assemble a group of photographs (five to ten, if possible) of a relative long dead—a grandparent or great-grandparent. By weaving in family stories and memories, and by looking closely at the photographs, have the student write a two- to three-page treatment on the person. The photographs should help them evoke emotion and detail, even if it turns out some of their conclusions are inaccurate. It can be critiqued by other family members.

Step 7: *Memoir prewriting exercise.* When students set out to write their own memoir piece, they begin to see more seriously the issues of boundaries. Traditionally, first-person writing was all done for a public setting. Secret diaries were for a private setting. But many writers these days bring more personal experiences and perspectives into the public through memoirs. Mini-activities here can include: Have students do quick writes or journal writes with the following prompts: "Something I could never write about is . . ." and "The hidden/secret reason for my [here list a habit or personal trait or achievement] is . . ." Students can either share or not share these quick writes. But the discussion will be about understanding how difficult it is to tell the truth, even about yourself, and how difficult it is to get access to someone else's internal thought process.

Step 8: *Memoir reading.* Have students read a few memoirs. The class can get short pieces out of the *New Yorker* or other magazines, or they can agree on a short book as an example. Consider a chapter out of

Nabokov's *Speak, Memory* or Anaïs Nin's *Diary*. Again, discuss the use of detail, the honesty with self and the reader, and issues of public and private domains of information.

Step 9: *Writing a memoir.* Next, students should attempt to write a short memoir, similar to the biographical sketches. This should be more crafted and intentional than a journal but less formal than an essay. Again, students can discuss and plan these in groups and present them as public readings, wall displays, or published works.

Step 10: *A memoir over time.* Another interesting exercise is to consider how one's life looks different at different times. Margaret Haley wrote three memoirs at three times in her life and each one tells a different story. Have students write a memoir sketch in three parts, each written at three different times in their lives, such as in fourth grade, in middle school, and now. Or you can have them do a memoir piece now, seal it, and open it (you could mail it to them) in five or ten years and write another then, to see how they have changed. Discuss the different views, on life and on philosophy, at each stage.

Step 11: *Evaluation.* Whatever parts of the lesson plan your class has done, it is important to evaluate the process at the end. Students should revisit the issues that were discussed in the lesson plan on reading biography. Some of these include authorial choices, objective fact vs. point of view, narrative approach, public and private stories, and status and power. What do the students understand about biography that they did not before? How do these insights apply to history, anthropology, literature? What more would the students want to explore to take this further?

Drama

LANGUAGE: AN EAR FOR THE VOICE
Lesson Plan No. 1

OVERVIEW: *Working* demands exploration far beyond the issues of work and careers. Terkel is a sociologist but he is also an artist and an actor. One of the most compelling aspects of his work is his aptitude for turning interviews into drama. In this unit, we will take some time to jump off from the book to issues of drama and language. I recognize the many controversies and complexities that this direction invites, but such issues can be engaged at the middle school and high school levels with great success. Some of the exercises here will help attune the students' ear to voices all around them. Others will take it deeper, to issues of language and power, to discourse and its purposes. In my experience, students always enjoy and remember these exercises.

Objectives for Students

- Recognize and learn to record the complexities of speech and communication.
- Become aware of their own discourse communities.
- Learn to translate between different discourse styles for different audiences.
- Write in different manners for different audiences.
- Analyze the subtext and multiple meanings in speech.

TIME: Because of the number of days needed to complete parts of this lesson plan, it will take about two weeks. But it will not require the use of all class time.

MATERIALS: Copies of excerpts from "Professor Seagull" in *Up in the Old Hotel* (1993) by Joseph Mitchell, *Fires in the Mirror* (1993) by Anna Deveare Smith, *The Real Ebonics Debate* (1998), edited by Theresa Perry and Lisa Delpit; video versions of Anna Deveare Smith's performances (on PBS). Devise other readings that are appropriate.

PROCEDURE:
Step 1: *Introducing the concept.* Share with students the following discussion. The renowned playwright and actress Anna Deveare Smith wrote in "The Shades of Loss,"

> For sixteen years now, inspired in part by the work of the great chronicler of American life, Mr. Studs Terkel, I have been searching for American character by using the tools of the theater. I have been creating performances based on actual events in a series entitled *On the Road: A Search for American Character*. Each *On the Road* performance evolves from interviews I conduct with individuals directly or indirectly involved in the event I intend to explore. . . . I am trying to give an account of what and how a person spoke with me. I believe that character lives in how a person speaks as well as in what they say, and in the inability to speak as well as in moments of fluid articulation. . . . The purpose of the work is to create dialogue, and to use the ambience and techniques of the theater to inspire discussion about the events of our time.

One of the best ways to encounter and extend the importance of Terkel's *Working* is on the stage. Stage productions that use parts of the book have been done for many years; one was even a musical. But as Anna Deveare Smith suggests, the "ambience and techniques" of the theater help to create a dialogue about our times.

Much of Terkel's work is art, seeking the core of the human spirit.

Teacher Frank Tobin has taught in a Chicago juvenile detention center for twenty years. He stays centered by reminding himself that there is God in every human being. No young offender is dismissed as trash, as the enemy, as the other. This God in the center of every human being is also what Studs Terkel looks for—and finds.

Terkel reports his findings in books and on the radio. They could be quite well reported on the stage. For the stage, however, we have to learn to pay even more attention to the nuance of voice, of body language, of spoken and unspoken meaning. Anna Deveare Smith, in her *On the Road* series, created *Fires in the Mirror* about the 1991 Crown Heights riots in Brooklyn, and then *Twilight: Los Angeles, 1992* about the beating of Rodney King. Her main writing aid was her tape recorder. She interviewed participants and observers, the famous and obscure. She then studied the tapes, meticulously, repeatedly, and worked to create the characters. Smith's one-woman shows consisted of performances of a wide range of characters: black, white, Orthodox Jewish, Muslim. One moment she would be a Beverly Hills matron, the next a youth from South Central Los Angeles. She points out that this is not simply "mimicry," but rather a theatrical attempt to evoke the whole cast of characters and each individual.

If possible, view video versions of Anna Deveare Smith's performances and discuss her method of creating drama and capturing voice.

Step 2: *Training the ear.* You can imagine the possibilities, creating drama from *Working,* using other transcribed texts, having students do their own interviews that lead to dramatic performance. But before that, have students do some exercises that prepare them. It is easy to enjoy Anna Deveare Smith but extremely difficult to imitate her art. In fact, years of theatrical training go into her ability to capture voice and character in her performances.

Instead of ten years of theatrical training, have students try some simpler steps. Have them imagine what it would be like to go around recording voices of everyone, creating a picture of the world as it is, and to imagine someone doing that, transcribing conversation, during the Civil War, in T'ang Dynasty China, in ancient Egypt. Inform them that there actually was a person who did this during the 1920s and '30s in New York, someone named Joe Gould. Gould was an eccentric, an early bohemian, and homeless guy who went around filling notebooks with an "oral history" of his time. He would sit and interview common folk for hours. He would write down overheard conversation. He would seek to get it exactly right. What a treasure trove of history he must have created! And a very insightful writer for the *New Yorker* got to know Joe Gould and wrote down his story.

Assign students to read "Professor Seagull," from *Up in the Old Hotel* (1993) by Joseph Mitchell. (This story is also told in the 2000 film release, *Joe Gould's Secret*, though the oral history issues are better presented in the original written version.)

Step 3: *Overheard conversation.* Discuss "Professor Seagull" and Joe Gould. In what ways was he a precursor to Studs Terkel? Where are his thousands of notebooks today? What kind of play could be made out of them? If Dorothea Lange was the visual chronicler of the Depression in the countryside, Joe Gould was the chronicler of those years in Greenwich Village in New York.

Tell students: Now we are going to try out our skills at this. We are going to be Joe Goulds of our time. The purpose of this exercise is to gain familiarity with vernacular speech, sometimes to even become aware of our own speech. For this exercise, you are not doing an interview. You are overhearing conversation. You are to find a comfortable and safe place to record conversation for 5 to 15 minutes. This is not to be done with a tape recorder but should be written rapidly. You should attempt to get inflections, patterns of speech, even body language and pauses. You will have three days to complete this. (Provide students with the information in "Writing Assignment No. 1.")

Step 4: *Awareness of discourse.* Students are to bring in their overheard conversations. Have a number of students read theirs aloud. They can try a few times to get it right, to capture the exact sounds. The idea of this exercise is not to ridicule how people talk but rather to come to appreciate their character and strength in use of the language. Ask: How many students sit in class and speak in one syllable answers, then break into a poetic flight of brilliance when teasing friends in the hall? What is the subtext in a conversation, the thing not being said? Are there multiple meanings in the conversation, expressed through subtleties of speech or through body language? As students realize the linguistic strengths of their own discourse and that of peers, then learn to bridge to other language conventions for different audiences, they can bring this

Writing Assignment No. 1:
OVERHEARD CONVERSATION

This is a much different writing assignment than any you have done. In fact, you are not going to write at all. You are going to overhear a conversation, basically eavesdrop on people talking. You will write down exactly what is said and try to write it the way it sounds. This is the process of capturing the "oral history of our times," much like Joe Gould did in New York in the 1930s. This writing exercise will be read in class as part of a discussion about the many voices, the many idioms, the many types of vernacular speech that exist in our complex society.

You may write your oral history notes anywhere you can hear people talking—on the bus, in the library, at a family reunion. But you must write exactly what you hear. It cannot be from TV (that is, a script). It can be in a language other than English (extra credit!) but you should then translate it so it can be shared.

Two pages, typed.

Due: _____

confidence and power of language into other forms of expression, even standard English.

The next assignment is designed to get students to think about their own discourse community, their own strengths of expression. (See "Writing Assignment No. 2.") They are to write a short paper using their own vernacular, whether it is ebonics, valley-speak, Spanglish (a mixture of Spanish and English decried by many Spanish teachers but embraced by many immigrant youths), etc. Sometimes students will surprise you and teach you something about their social experience; I have heard Laotian teens in East Oakland, new immigrants just learning English, joke with friends in what we would call ebonics, because they were learning English in the predominant African-American neighborhood.

When I first gave this assignment, I was certain it would create instant articulate scholars because I was giving them permission to write as they speak with friends, informally. But, while it is still a great assignment because it encourages metacognition, thinking about one's thinking, and wisdom about discourse communities, it is a struggle for most students to write the way they talk with friends.

Students will need some reassurance to feel comfortable with this assignment. And of course some will insist that they already speak "standard English." But most will find an idiom and style they can slide into. Be aware that if they are given license to write this way, they will also use obscenities. Whether to allow that is each teacher's call.

Step 5: *The power of language.* Have students bring in their creations. Some will have enjoyed the task and some will have suffered. But all should participate in oral reading of sections and in evaluation and discussion. Tell the students that you are not looking for who has the most daring or the most strange story. Make it a discussion about language. Remind them that language is never a static set of rules. Shakespeare himself was inventing words, creating combinations of various vernaculars, and breaking old rules when he wrote his plays. Only with the nineteenth-century zeal for scientific management did language and grammar become prescriptive and forbidding. Tell them you are looking for the writing that captures some heart, some core of feeling—the brilliance and inventiveness of the language.

Again, as with the interviews, students begin to find out things about themselves when they explore their language. Terkel says in his intro-

Writing Assignment No. 2:
REFLECTIONS IN VERNACULAR

Write a brief description of something you have accomplished in school this year, academically and/or socially. This is to be written entirely in your own vernacular or home language. This can be Spanish, Chinese, Farsi; it can be teenage lingo or the language of teenage note-passing. It is not to be standard English. Think about examples of vernacular writing—the overheard conversations you wrote up, Joe Gould's notebooks, the works of Anna Deveare Smith and Studs Terkel, as well as first person narrations in novels like *Youth in Revolt, The Bluest Eye, Catcher in the Rye*, and *Sapphire.*

Before you begin to write, think seriously for a while about the subject. You do not have to survey everything that is happening in your life. You may zero in on one aspect, one story, one situation. But make sure that you put some real thought into this story, so you are revealing new insights you have gained or a new determination you have reached or something deep and interesting about the experience.

Two pages, typed.

Due: _____

duction to *Working*, "On one occasion, during a play-back, my companion murmured in wonder, 'I never realized I felt that way.' And I was filled with wonder, too" (p. xix). How often do we discover ourselves as we hear our words come back to us?

Step 6: *Ebonics and power.* If there is time, you can put in here a study and discussion of the debate on ebonics. This was something that broke out in earnest when the Oakland (California) Unified School District announced that it was going to provide instruction in ebonics (also known as "Black English") to African-American children. The idea here was to honor students' home language while introducing them to standard English. But of course the pundits jumped in with narrow opinions about the problems of African-American achievement and the cultural deprivation of African-American communities. Avoiding for the moment the distinction between a "language" and a "dialect," we can certainly agree that a standard language is a dialect with an army. That is, those in power determine what the standard language is. Noah Webster wrote his American dictionary in 1806 as an act of nationalism, to distinguish how we speak from the allegedly superior British. America's "army" was becoming stronger and we needed to standardize our way of speaking.

One of the more calm and developed discussions of the language skills issues at stake is in *The Real Ebonics Debate* (1998), edited by Theresa Perry and Lisa Delpit. Students can research this debate and re-create it. One of the best articles on the subject is Lisa Delpit's "What Should Teachers Do? Ebonics and Culturally Responsive Instruction," in the same anthology.

Step 7: *Translate to Standard English.* If the idea of this exercise is to honor students' discourse communities—make them aware of them and help them to bridge to other ways of speaking with other audiences—then the next step is to create an exercise in which students "translate" their vernacular writing (see Writing Assignment No. 3). The idea here is not to reject "standard English" but rather to have students become adept at using it at the appropriate time. Encourage students to become more literate and more powerful not just by mastering standard English but by learning to express themselves in a number of dialects and in knowing how to switch between them for various situations. Students will need three or four days to complete this assignment.

Writing Assignment, No. 3:
TRANSLATE TO STANDARD ENGLISH

Use your own vernacular or home language to write a brief description of something you have achieved or accomplished this year, academically and/or socially.

Now you are to **translate** that essay into "standard English." Whereas your style and diction were breezy and casual before, you now have to try to render the same story into the forms that would be acceptable in a college application essay. That means there should be an introduction, a body section that supports your argument, and a conclusion. You should correct grammar and spelling errors.

Remember, you are showing you can make the **same point** to two different audiences.

Two pages, typed.

Due: _____

Step 8: *Evaluation.* Write on the board the following quotation from Anna Deveare Smith on the power of the theater:

> The performance is a document of what an actress heard in Los Angeles. When I did my research in Los Angeles, I was listening with an ear that was trained to hear stories for the specific purpose of repeating them with the elements of character intact. This becomes significant because sometimes there is the expectation that inasmuch as I am doing "social dramas," I am looking for solutions to social problems. In fact, though, I am looking at the process of becoming something. It is not a result, it is not an answer. It is not a solution. I am first looking for the humanness inside the problems or the crises. The spoken word is evidence of that humanness. The aliveness of the theater is also an affirmation of that humanness. Perhaps the solutions lie in part in the humanness of the audience, and in the potential for dialogue and action after the curtain goes down. (from "The Shades of Loss")

Have students bring in their papers and read them, sharing the struggles they went through to do the translation. Ask: Why is it important to speak in standard English in some situations? Why is it inappropriate to employ that style in others?

We have looked in this lesson at how people talk in our society. Especially since we live in such a diverse society, students are exposed to dozens of ways of speaking, of being articulate and inventive. Have students discuss (or write quick responses): What have we learned about language in this process? What kinds of details should you look for in studying a person's oral testimonial? What have you learned about your own way of speaking?

PERFORMANCE: THE HUMAN DRAMA
Lesson Plan No. 2

OVERVIEW: Now, students will have reflected on issues of oral history and interview techniques. This drama lesson is a performance, a chance for students to bring together insights they have gained and show what they can do with them. This is a way to make the understanding deeper and make it relevant and accessible to future situations students will face—in school and in the world.

Objectives for Students

- Evaluate elements of language necessary to tell a story.
- Work as a group to develop a theme and a script.
- Develop listening skills as well as acting skills for performance.
- Evaluate the performance and literary insights gained.

TIME: From one to four weeks,

MATERIALS: Classroom set of *Working*; a copy of *The Oral History Reader* (Perks and Thomson); props and materials for performance (depending on staging, this might include tape recorders, video cameras and monitors, stage sets, costumes, and so on).

PROCEDURE:

Step 1: *Introduction to drama.* Many great writers who were expert at capturing vernacular speech were interviewers in the Depression for the Federal Writers' Project, including Zora Neale Hurston, John Cheever, Ralph Ellison, Saul Bellow, Richard Wright, and May Swenson.

The idea of developing a stage performance from the transcribed words of others is not new. We have looked at the work of Anna Deveare Smith and considered issues of vernacular and language. Courtroom dramas are also made up of taped transcripts. And students have created plays from Studs Terkel's *Working*, as well as from his *Division Street: America* and *Hard Times.*

One of the famous productions by the Federal Theater Project in the 1930s was the creation of drama from real life. The actors and writers spent two months poring over the newspaper, studying the news of the day. Then they created a theatrical piece that was current and reflected issues of the day. The government shut down the play after three performances.

Have students imagine the different ways that staging can be done. Discuss how oral history and voice-of-the-people approaches demand consideration of ways to break the "fourth wall" in theater, to interact with the audience. At Michigan-Flint University, a group called the Labor Theater Project recently created a play on the famous Flint sit-down strike against General Motors in 1936–37. The audience walked into the theater, which had been transformed into a factory, and found itself wandering among groups of workers, inside and outside of the factory. The script was taken from recent interviews as well as tapes made at the time of the strike. (See "Out of the Archives and onto the Stage" by Shaun Nethercott and Neil Leighton, in *The Oral History Reader*, edited by Robert Perks and Alistair Thomson, New York: Routledge, 1998.) Read aloud excerpts from this performance which appear in the article.

Also describe how, a few years ago in San Francisco, a play was produced on the top floor of a large parking garage. The actors all sat in automobiles, talking with friends, lovers, family members. Some of the text was ad-libbed, some was written, some was remembered from overheard conversations or interviews. The audience walked around among the automobiles, listening to dialogue, watching the interactions, strangely being at the same time voyeurs and participants.

Step 2: *Brainstorming.* Discuss ways to create an oral history drama. Have students decide on one theme or question and develop the drama around that. It could be an area of work—for example, slaughterhouse workers on the outside of town—or it could be local history, that of a neighborhood, the account of a local strike, etc. Sometimes it is best to pursue a particular theme—for example, women and body image: What are the media messages? What are the views of women? Or the theme could be racism, or homophobia.

Or it could just be about teen life at school. In some ways, school life is a strong area to mine and it is the one the students know the best. Yet you might decide that it is important to move students out of their world, to use this assignment to introduce the larger community and interact with it. In creating this drama, students move from being passive readers of community life to active participants.

Decide on the organizing principle of the performance and begin to plan how to conduct, collect, and edit the interviews necessary to create a script.

Step 3: *Listening to the language.* Students should now go out and gather raw material. This can be a series of interviews (see Interview Techniques Unit starting on p. 3) mixed with overheard conversations. Again, if students have the final performance in mind when they conduct the interviews, they will direct their interviews to that end. Anna Deveare Smith consulted a linguist when she started *On the Road*. She wanted to learn how to listen for the breakdown of syntax. The linguist gave her a set of questions to ask, which were: (1) Have you ever come close to death? (2) Have you ever been accused of something you did not do? and (3) Do you remember the circumstances of your birth? (See *Fires in the Mirror*, by Anna Deveare Smith, p. xxxix.) These questions in themselves—or ones like them—could become the focus of an investigation. She says they taught her how to listen. She also found that one incredible interview subject in New York's Crown Heights, Carmel Cato, actually answered all three of those questions without being asked. Deveare says, "Many people are answering one, if not all, of those questions. I don't ask those questions, but it comes up in many interviews. People have come close to death; they do feel accused of something that they didn't do, whether it's being apprehended by the police for no other reason than being the wrong color in the wrong neighborhood, or because of the fear people have of being in any neighborhood at any time. Many people do remark on the circumstances of their 'cultural' birth, their original nationality, their ethnicity. American character is alive inside of syntactical breaks."

Students can also consult works by performer Danny Hoch, who has also created characters from people he encounters, knows, or listens to. He talks about the need to have a "photogenic ear," one that picks up the nuances and inflections that reveal everything about the character.

Step 4: *Creating a script.* The biggest job is sharing the interviews and organizing them into a coherent piece, a script. Students can write sections as needed for transitions and clarity. The class becomes familiar with the script by reading it aloud, again and again. Critique should serve to help the readers get the words right and capture the subtext and subtle meanings.

Ask students: What is your organizing center? By this I don't mean the theme but rather the visual, physical presence that runs through the play. Is it a narrator who wanders through the action like the narrator in Wilder's *Our Town*? Oral history drama provides a wonderful opportunity for students to experiment with Brecht's techniques: breaking the fourth wall, creating audience reflection by using signs or large projections to introduce scene changes and actors addressing the audience either in character or as themselves, as well as introducing critique of the drama during the play itself.

What is the dramatic structure? How is the theme introduced? How is it built to a peak of understanding and insight? How is the denouement, the final reflection and closing, constructed? This is where major editing work is done by the group.

Once the group decides on a theme for the play, they have to commit to that theme and stick to it. Often they are tempted to change the plan entirely when encountering obstacles and frustrations. But once a plan is agreed to, the energy needs to go into making it work.

Step 5: *Casting.* Casting is another of the major hurdles in setting up a theatrical performance. This is not a stage that should be rushed or done arbitrarily by the teacher. Establishing roles and who will perform them is a task for the whole class. Some will leave casting open for a while, during which time readings and practices begin. This way, the class has time to see certain actors grow into a character.

Step 6: *Staging the play.* In working with oral history material, sometimes classes will create mini-plays to be shown just to the class or to a few other classes. Other times this project becomes a major production.

Staging depends on how and when you are going to perform the piece. Is the physical space a standard theater with a stage, or a warehouse? Inside or outside? Consider unique approaches such as the car-talk play or the Flint sit-down strike play. Remember, however, that the staging should serve to make the spirit and ideas of the play come across more powerfully, not to be clever for its own sake.

Consider other options. This can be made into a wonderful radio play, done through "real time" performance on tape or through a performance broken into bits and edited. It can also be a video, made for the class or for broadcast on local TV or cable. This allows more staging options; you can set one scene in a certain part of town, another scene in another.

Stage 7. *Evaluation.* Depending on the kind of performance the class puts on, the evaluation will be more or less elaborate. It is important, however, to reflect on what students learned in the unit. Although at this point students will mostly want a cast party, they will also want to talk about insights they gained and ways they think the performance could be made better. The public at the performance, whether it is community members or other students, should also be asked to fill out feedback forms that can be read by the group and considered. Students can even write their own theatrical reviews of the performance.

Then students should be able to come back to issues raised in this whole unit, on language and power, subtext and multiple meanings. And they should be able to think about the meaning of *Working* and oral history.

New Economics

RESEARCH IN ECONOMICS
Lesson Plan No. 1

OVERVIEW: Many teachers use *Working* as a resource for an economics course or in school-to-career curricula. The activities described in these two lesson plans are some of the ways you can make that connection. Studs Terkel paints a portrait of the economy from the bottom up, from a perspective that is more interesting and engaging to many students than traditional lessons in economics, which Thomas Carlyle called "the dismal science."

In this set of activities, students will learn to do economic research. In the next set, they will incorporate some journalistic and oral interview activities. You may choose to branch into a complex study of the world economy today or you may simply help students visualize and investigate their own employment options.

Objectives for Students

- Develop research skills on economics and employment.
- Analyze the workings of the world market today.
- Survey community employment options.
- Plan and investigate career options.

TIME:
Four days to two weeks.

MATERIALS: Copies of *Working*, access to library facilities and local agencies.

PROCEDURE:

Step 1: *Introduction.* Terkel paints a portrait of the economy in 1972: how things were manufactured and moved around, services were provided, and people lived. He also described a range of jobs available to high school graduates in 1972. Ask students if they think they could get those same jobs today. Which are gone or greatly diminished? What new jobs exist that did not exist before?

Since 1972, we have seen massive changes in the economy due to globalization and the information age. The new economy looks quite different from the one Studs Terkel described. This section investigates how and why those changes happened and looks into the kinds of jobs and careers students can expect to encounter today.

Step 2: *Research assignment* No. 1. (For individuals or groups.) Students are to create a profile of the book *Working* and describe the range of jobs that exist according to the book. While Studs Terkel was not intending to do a scientific profile of the economy, he tried to include everyone. Have students create categories as follows: white collar (management), blue collar (manufacturing), service (from sales to fast food), professional (doctors, lawyers), and government (including police, fire, and education). Also, have them divide the jobs by low pay, middle pay, and high pay.

Next, have them look at data from 1970 or 1974. This can be found in many sources, including Census data and the Bureau of Labor Statistics (http://stats.bls.gov). What was the real profile of the economy? This time, students should be able to break down the pay level of the workforce more precisely, starting with the percent making less than $15,000, on up. They can make visual representations, charts, or other pictures to show the shape of the economy.

Step 3: *Reading.* Have the students read the "Demon Lover" section of *Working* (Book Four). What are the different jobs in the automobile industry? How do the workers in these jobs complement each other and compete with each other? Have them look at another area of the economy: What are the different jobs in that industry? How do they work in relation to each other? What jobs are desirable and why?

Step 4: *Research assignment No. 2.* Have students update the data from Step 2. What are the latest statistics they can find? Have job categories changed? What about income and income differential (the difference between the lowest and the highest)? Have them create a visual way to illustrate the shape of the new workforce, placing the current economic profile next to the one created for 1972. Now have them answer a question that could not be answered above: What jobs from *Working* are virtually gone? What are new jobs that did not exist then? Have students describe the economic character of modern industrial society: Who digs and builds? How many resources are devoted to public work, government, the professions, education? Does employment (in different categories, by pay level) break down along racial lines? Why? What is their prediction for the direction the economy will develop in the future?

Besides the main statistical resources in the library, institutions like the National Center for Research in Vocational Education (Berkeley), Autodesk Foundation (San Rafael), and Jobs for the Future (Boston) can be consulted. (See Resource Guide, pp. 193–197.)

Step 5: *Mini-lecture and discussion.* Discuss the following issues with your students: Recent changes in the economy are the result of a new organization of the economy on a world scale, known as globalization. Companies used to exist in one country or another and compete with each other; now companies span the globe. These changes are the result of many new conditions: increased efficiency of transportation and communication; the downfall of the former Soviet Union and the end of the Cold War; the search for cheaper labor, thus moving manufacturing to poorer countries; and the expansion of computer technology. (See *Field Guide to the Global Economy* by Sarah Anderson et al., New York: The New Press, 1999.)

During the first two-thirds of the twentieth century, the U.S. economy also functioned as part of a world economy, but it was organized differently. In the old model, raw materials were dug up, farmed, and mined in the underdeveloped parts of the world in Asia, Africa, and Latin America, once known as the Third World—after the capitalist West and the socialist East. (These regions are now euphemistically called the "developing countries." Whether and how they are developing is yet to be seen.) Their raw materials were brought into the industrial centers of Europe, North America, and Japan, where everything from automobiles to toasters was manufactured. This was the period in which the blue-collar workers dominated such large industrial centers as Detroit and Chicago.

Since 1970, however, manufacturing and factory work had also moved to the Third World. By the end of the 1980s, the last television factory operated by an American company in the U.S. was sold to the Korean corporation Samsung. After two years, it moved the plant to Tijuana, Mexico.[1] This trend has serious implications for the working life of people in these new industrial regions of the world as well as for workers in the U.S.

Here's how the situation was explained by the American director of a high-tech auto facility in Mexico: "His engines, he bragged, were the product of 'U.S. managers, European technology, Japanese manufacturing systems, and Mexican workers.' " Of course, this rosy picture does not mention a key point: the bulk of the profit goes to U.S. corporations, even though there are no U.S. workers in the picture.[2]

This perspective is important for students to keep in mind. Often you hear that information and computers are the key to the economy today. The creation of computer models has allowed corporations to do much more efficient accounting and planning than in the past. And indeed information systems and computers are where you will find many jobs in the U.S. But this does not mean that manufacturing has disappeared. It is just that factory work has moved to other countries, to regions we often don't see in our world.

And because there is a world of workers to choose from, and because markets are "opened up" so companies can move orders and products to any part of the globe, there is the problem of the "race to the bottom." In other words, if you can pay a worker $1.50 an hour in Korea, that is where you want to be. But if then you find out that you can pay a worker $0.82 per day in Burma, you just might make another move.

This is not a linear or simple process, however. While manufacturing raced overseas in the '80s and early '90s, many companies found that the support and maintenance needed for overseas plants overshadowed

---

[1]Steve Brouwer, *Sharing the Pie: A Citizen's Guide to Wealth and Power in America*, New York: Henry Holt, 1998.
[2]Steve Brouwer, *Prosperity Lost*, Reading, MA: Addison-Wesley, 1990.

the profits generated by low wages. So there has been a countertrend of factories moving back to the U.S.

For now, such moves mean fantastic profits inside the U.S., profits that are held by the very rich but also shared with many in the middle class. People are stunned to see the value of their stocks rising so fast. Someone who invested their 401(k) retirement money in the stock market five years ago may have seen it triple in value by now. The explosion of the NASDAQ stock listings, which depend more on information companies than other listings, the instant riches in the "dot-com" sector—all give the illusion that wealth is just springing out of the ground and everyone should jump on the bandwagon. The question is: Will these profits continue? Will a carnival of riches and goods produced by super-poor countries continue to make our tables groan with resources? Where will it all go?

And more immediately, what is the impact on labor markets and working conditions in the U.S. as a result of the acceleration of technological change and globalization? Now there are many more technology and computer jobs. But without a manufacturing core, you find a big gap between the well-paid computer jobs and the service jobs at the bottom. How many teens find their only option to be flipping burgers at the local McDonald's? Many from your students' generation know the service sector is the most likely option for employment. Young people say, "I'm in retail" or "I'm in fast food," and everyone knows their dilemma. Movies like *Clerks* describe young people employed at dead-end service jobs.

My father was a Chicago industrialist, a "captain of industry." He delighted in the fact that Chicago's economy rested on a solid foundation of manufacturing, of factories. That was the rock core of the economy. I once mentioned during the '70s that I was thinking of moving to New Orleans. "New Orleans?" he grimaced. "Why, everybody there is just taking out each other's laundry." What did he mean by that? He meant that there was no basic manufacturing at the core of the economy, that most of the economy was based on services. But when people are just performing services for each other, who is creating the basic wealth? Nobody. So the economy is weak, shaky, likely to have a downturn. My father is absolutely shocked today to see how much manufacturing has moved out of the United States to the Third World. Now in the U.S., everybody is taking out each other's laundry.

What are the implications for stability? What if these workers around the world, who now have their hands on the core manufacturing plants, were to strike, to rebel, to take them over? Perhaps that's why the United States maintains its massive military machine and active presence around the world, even though the Cold War is over. Military spending, in this view, is not just a boondoggle to spend taxpayers' money. It is to protect the flow of goods, to protect the control of the factories, against the danger of revolution.

What are the implications for our community structure? Right now, there are many wealthy communities that thrive on the profits of the world economy, but the workers who are employed to get them their meals, make their cappuccinos, and wash their clothes cannot afford to live nearby and need to commute long distances.

One of the most important observations Studs Terkel makes about work in his book concerns alienation, in the Marxist sense of the word. In a complex economy, the worker is alienated from the product of his/her labor. Whereas over most of human history a person made a product and immediately saw the end result (say, a pair of shoes, or an ax), in a complex economy the worker is on the job all day but never sees the finished product and is not part of the final product. So the worker is alienated (separated) from the product and also from a sense of community. All kinds of social ills result from this type of production. Studs Terkel put it this way in his interview for this book (see p. 148): "Sometimes work, you know, is a chore. For many people that's so. Now the assembly line worker, thanks to the UAW, is thirty and out. Thirty years and then you get a pension. And he dreams, oh, he longs for the time he can be thirty and out, and he can go fishing, he can take it easy, to go. What does he do all day at work? He shoots that welding gun and all day, twenty pounds or so, all day in one spot, into a revolving snake, the assembly line. He doesn't see the end product. And we know that in Sweden they have teams that do the car from beginning to end."

Ask students: Do you think that the new economy, the world economy, has lessened the alienation of the typical worker in the U.S.? What about the typical worker in the newly industrialized zones? Why?

In today's economy, planning and production are usually organized around teams. Whereas the old factory model demanded that workers be disciplined and follow instructions, today's employees are expected to work together, to think "outside the box," and to have the final product and goal in mind at each stage of production. In a sense, modern managers want to lessen the "alienation of labor" and give each worker a stake in the outcome. How might you see this operating in today's economy? How does this suggest what we should do to redesign education for students? Remind students that this is clearly an opinionated overview of the developments in the economy since 1972. Have them do their own research to draw their own conclusions.

Step 6: *Research assignment No. 3, investigating your own community.* Have students consult the business editor of their local newspaper and speak to local employment and welfare officials. Have them draw a picture of the kinds of economic activities in the community and the kinds of jobs available. Have them investigate real enterprises and institutions in the community and look at the service jobs and at what kind of job satisfaction they provide. If it is a visual representation (chart, wall display) similar to the ones above on the economy in 1972 and today, have them displayed next to each other.

Have students create a booklet for the community about its economy and career options. This can be displayed at Chamber of Commerce and employment offices as well as in the school's career office.

Step 7: *School to career.* Students can develop a plan for their own education and job experiences based on the surveys described here. Have students write their own "ten-year plan." This plan would include great detail about the college or career track the student is planning. It should go beyond simply saying, "I hope to attend state college." Students can explore that college, read the course outlines, and plan four years of classes he/she would take. If the student says, "I plan to work in construction," he/she should go to a site, talk to the foreman, and find out what preparation is needed. The exercise of creating a ten-year plan is an important step in grounding in reality students' expectations about their futures.

There are many resources to be consulted in this search, such as *Teaching the New Basic Skills: Proposals for Educating Children to Thrive in a Changing Economy*, by Frank Levy and Richard Murnane (New York: Free Press, 1996).

INTERVIEWS IN ECONOMICS
Lesson Plan No. 2

OVERVIEW: After students have completed research on the economy, they can use skills developed in the Interview and Oral History units to go out and create a profile of local career options. This makes the study of economics more realistic and accessible.

It is not enough to re-create the typical, usually boring, pamphlets found in many career offices. Students need to get out there and meet real people on the job, to have a chance to consider the good, the bad, and the ugly.

Conducting interviews along with economic investigation is engaging for students, partly because it is an activity away from the isolation of high school life and partly because it is a chance to check out the real world. You may want to organize seminars and study groups linking academic skills to local community work.

This lesson is particularly relevant for students in school-to-career programs and academies. Students working in job settings as interns and apprentices can broaden their reflection on their experience through this survey and interview process.

Objectives for Students

- Understand and evaluate the functioning of the local and global economy.
- Learn methods to investigate the economy.
- Extend interview skills.
- Recognize the importance of community service in doing research and investigation.

If I and other teachers truly want to provoke our students to break through the limits of the conventional and the taken-for-granted, we ourselves have to experience breaks with what has been established in our own lives; we have to keep arousing ourselves to begin again.

—Maxine Greene, *Existential Encounters for Teachers* and
The Dialectics of Learning

TIME: One to three weeks, depending on organization. This can also be taught in conjunction with the Research in Economics activity.

MATERIALS: Local resources for job investigation, tape recorders, materials necessary for publishing.

PROCEDURE:

Step 1: *Review and plan.* Students should review the research they have done on the local economy and local career options. What kind of Terkel-type investigation would be useful to further this research? Instead of looking only at data, tell students to meet the people behind the data and plan a series of interviews as a class with an eye to publishing a more comprehensive local job guide. Students can interview individuals in all the major job categories in the community; they can interview people in careers they hope to enter—the ones they've named in their ten-year plans.

Another way to organize a series of interviews is to find people in a shrinking job category—for example, factory work. Have students interview such a person and compare this interview to ones in *Working* for a similar job. Students can also compare the experience of workers in a particular job category today and in 1972. This comparison can be done in a written report, in an oral report to the class, in a video presentation, and numerous other ways (see "Publishing" below, step 6).

A variation of this is to find jobs that did not exist in 1972—such as many computer programming and information tech jobs—and to interview people in those categories. Has job satisfaction, a sense of fulfillment and agency, increased for workers in these new categories compared to 1972? How do people find their dreams, and hopes, in these new jobs?

Discuss work opportunities for teens in the local community. What would it take to go beyond pamphlets found in career centers, to create something useful for teens looking for work? Can the class compile a report with real information on the jobs, the local history, labor struggles, and the ups and downs in the job market?

Step 2: *Guests.* During the course of this investigation, try to arrange to bring in guest speakers to the class. You can bring two or three at once or have one guest per week. People in the community are delighted to come into the school to share their stories. It is important to prepare the students for the visit, discuss proper respect for the guest, and discuss what questions to ask. The guest speaker can tell about his/her job, how he/she got it, things that are satisfying, and things that are frustrating. After the guest leaves, take some time to sum up the experience, asking students what they've learned about interviewing, and what new questions they want to ask when they go out in the community.

Step 3: *Interviews.* Students can use the Interview Techniques Unit to develop a plan for interviewing people in the community. Depending on the parameters the class has defined in the planning stage, students will take on interview assignments, focused on people in all different jobs in the community, or on people in jobs each student hopes to pursue. Students should go through the process of planning, sharing their ten questions with peers, testing the tape recorder, etc., in order to get the most effective interview.

Step 4: *Seminar.* During the interview process, the class can hold seminar discussions on issues related to the changing economy and changing job market. Seminars can rely on shared readings or even clippings from the newspaper. Students can do research for the seminar discussion by speaking to other experts in the community. They should bring this information in to the seminars for discussion. If you are holding academic discussions on the subject while the interview process is going on, the interviews will inform the academic work and the academic work will strengthen the interviews.

Step 5: *Job shadowing.* One of the best ways to follow up the interview is to shadow the subject at his/her job. In some situations, a "shadow" may stay in the background and say nothing; in other situations, he/she participates. This all depends on everyone's comfort level. The important thing is that the student keep notes, write journal im-

DISCUSSION QUESTIONS AND ACTIVITIES TO ACCOMPANY *WORKING*

Introduction

The introduction to *Working* visits themes and issues carried throughout the book. It is useful to have the class read a section of the book, discuss it, and come back to the introduction for Studs Terkel's view on these issues.

Have students make a list of new and unfamiliar references. Research and discuss: What is "Orwellian acceptance," or "Luddite sabotage"? Look up and read the writings of Henry Mayhew (see *Working*, p. xiii), Thomas Carlyle, Charles Dickens, Samuel Beckett, Horatio Alger, and photographer Walker Evans.

This section of the teaching guide consists of discussion questions for use in the classroom, and proven activities that correspond to different sections of Studs Terkel's *Working*. These evolved from brainstorming and teacher-sharing models. For more extensively developed lesson plans, see Section I.

The Prefaces

Working includes three prefaces. Divide the class into three groups and have them each read one. Have the groups present to the rest of the class the main theme in each preface. How has Terkel grouped these interviews?

Find the entire text of Brecht's "A Worker Reads History" that introduces the first preface (quoted on p. xxxi) in *Selected Poems of Bertolt Brecht*, edited by H. R. Hays, New York: Grove Press, 1959. Read and discuss with the class. Read other Brecht poems and discuss.

Steelworker Mike Lefevre (Preface I) starts off by saying, "I'm a dying breed." Have students research steel and industrial work in the 1970s. How many such jobs existed in the United States in the 1970s? In the 2000s?

Young boys used to have newspaper delivery routes, as described in Preface II. Discuss how many do that now. Who delivers newspapers today? What do young kids do for jobs today?

When reading the interview with Carl Murray Bates in Preface III, have students consider the dignity of labor and the way human dreams and aspirations can be tied up with one's job. What core values and passions does Bates express? How does this apply to other jobs?

Book One: Working the Land

DISCUSSION QUESTIONS

How do family farms fare today? What is the role of the family farm in American myth and tradition? How are family farms preserved today?

What kind of portrait of mining life does Studs Terkel draw? Compare these accounts with the film *Harlan County, U.S.A.*, directed by Barbara Kopple.

What are the health and environmental implications of strip-mining?

ACTIVITIES

In his introduction, Studs Terkel refers to Richard Hoggart's 1957 study, *The Uses of Literacy*, because it is one of the great modern meditations on school and work. He describes the "illuminating gesture" which reflects the work life a person has had. Students can picture such gestures in the description of the room of Katherine Haynes on page 14.

Discuss the following with students: When you think about your own situation, for the greatest part of your life your "job" has been to be a student. In the life of the student, there may be a struggle with authority, the problem of boredom and endurance, and issues of alienation. Richard Rodriguez, author of *Hunger of Memory* (Boston: D. R. Godine, 1982), also refers to Hoggart's study as he remembers his development as a student. In fact, Rodriguez found that as he became more proficient as a student, he also became alienated from his working class immigrant family.

After students have read Book One of *Working*, have them read the chapter "The Achievement of Desire" in *Hunger of Memory*. Discuss his struggles with his family and his thinking process (called "metacognition"). How does this compare with Katherine Haynes and Joe and Susie Haynes? How do they think of their lives?

Then have students write a reflective essay on "My education and Rodriguez's."

> This writing assignment will allow you to explore some of the issues we have discussed while reading the essay by Richard Rodriguez. You have spent most of your life in school. Describe your education thus far. Has it been mainly enjoyable? Has it been a negative experience? Have you faced a crisis of confidence or a major hurdle? Do you find that you have to change, to break with traditions from your home culture, in order to succeed at school?
>
> Use concrete incidents, moments in time, to illustrate your point. These are more effective than generalizations. Make at least one reference to something Rodriguez says, whether your experience is similar to his or different. For example: "Just as Richard Rodriguez said, when he was in second grade, page xxx, I was . . ." or, "Unlike Richard Rodriguez, who found that . . . on page yyy . . ."
>
> The essay does not have to be long (a few pages is adequate), but it should be typed, free of spelling errors, and easy to understand.

This essay project is a great launching point for self-awareness discussions. As students perform activities in school, they can also be thinking critically about themselves as students and about issues of alienation and agency. We often come back in discussions to issues of alienation and students will say, "Well, like Rodriguez said . . ." as part of our normal discourse. Jamaica Kincaid's *Annie John* (1985) is another important text for comparison, inviting students to write their own short story about school life, enriching it with the insights of themselves as students/workers.

Book Two: Communications; A Pecking Order; Did You Ever Hear the One About the Farmer's Daughter?; The Commercial

DISCUSSION QUESTIONS

Heather Lamb says, "I'm a communications person but I can't communicate" (p. 36). What are the frustrations the receptionist and switchboard operator face? How have automated answering menus changed this situation for the better? For worse?

Terkel points out that during the Depression, people did not complain about their jobs; they were happy to have work. But, he says, Terry Mason (the airline stewardess) "has more spunk." What does he mean by this?

Look up what Sharon Atkins means by "Pavlov's bell" (p. 32). How has work changed the way you interact at home? Observe and report similar conditioned responses in yourself and in your parents or other workers.

Why do you suppose Terkel decided to put the hooker (p. 57) in the same group with the model, secretary, and airline stewardess?

How do advertisers manipulate media? What developments have there been in advertising since 1970?

Are there still installment dealers operating in cities? What niche in the economy does this person fill?

ACTIVITIES

Many of the speakers in this book are women. This is a good starting point for an investigation of gender and power. Joan Sangster (in *The Oral History Reader*, p. 87) writes about oral history being important for women because traditional forms of recording lives have ignored the disempowered. The publishing world is not as accessible to women. Ask students to think about the metaphor of the cookbook in Laura Esquivel's *Like Water for Chocolate*, the women's place where secrets and stories were kept, or of communities of women around a quilting table.

Students can read and critique the stories of women in "Communications" or "A Pecking Order." This can lead them to their own interviews and thematic investigations of female students at the school, older women in the community, or even of something more narrowly defined. Many such investigations are going on. For example, the city of Richmond, California, is doing a Rosie the Riveter project, interviewing women who worked in the shipyards during World War II.

Another theme that can be explored through this section is media literacy. Through these characters, we get a chance to look "behind the screen" in the world of sales and commercials. Since the publication of *Working*, of course, commercials have become more sophisticated and so have consumers. Young people generally tend to think of themselves as media-savvy and sophisticated. Today they are bombarded with messages that make fun of commercials in order to sell things, for example, a Sprite commercial wherein a man is portrayed as attractive to women because he drinks Sprite, while a voiceover proceeds to instruct viewers not to "believe the hype," to "just follow your thirst," and with scathing media deconstructions, such as the 1997 movie *Wag the Dog*. Does this mean that young consumers are strong critical thinkers? No, it means they have become cynical. Many young people reject critical reflection and community-oriented media as corny, and it is no longer enough to teach media literacy by showing the simple manipulations behind an advertisement.

There are many media literacy videos and lesson plans in the world today for your use. (See the Resource Guide.) Further ways to extend the discussion of this section include:

- Having students pursue interviews and investigations of local media outlets and talk to news reporters from radio, TV, and newspapers.
- Assigning students to time the local evening news hour. How many seconds are devoted to ads, to sports, to murder and mayhem, to political news, to international news, etc.? Have them bring in their data and add it up, generating a pie chart. Discuss choices the media make about coverage.
- Having students create their own media. The "Zine" phenomenon is an explosion of youth viewpoint—youth-created personal publications. Here you force students to grapple with what they want to say (see Zine assignment, pp. 102–105).
- Having students make their own video program for cable access, if you have the technical capacity at school. It can be made up of short news segments. Students can also make a presentation of life in their community through digital media. Even some students in elementary schools are making presentations on CD-ROM or creating stories that use hypertext (on-line programs that allow you to go to other sections for in-depth coverage). The same types of presentations can be made on Web pages.
- Having students interview people in media and in advertising who are doing work not even conceived of in 1972, when *Working* came out.

Make Your Own Zine

This project allows you to create your own Zine.

Why a Zine? Well, this may be the last, best form of free expression in journalism. With the demise of independent newspapers and the corporatization even of publications written for youth, Zines have arisen as a form of protest and creativity. In a Zine, you get to express your own opinion, show the many facets of yourself, and try out something new.

Does this mean that it is simply something *for* yourself? Not at all. A Zine is not an exercise in self-centeredness. You still have to reach an *audience*. You are still trying to *communicate* with someone.

After we have examined other Zines, you will begin working on your own versions. The format will be as follows: Take two 8½-by-14-inch pieces of paper and fold them in half. By inserting one in the other, you have created an eight-page paper whose pages are 7 by 8½ inches.

Your Zine should have:

- A cover that includes its name and a masthead. You may choose to put some text on the cover that explains your overall theme or approach, or you can just have art on the cover.

- A story of at least two pages in length. This story is to be actual news, something you dig up, something you find out. You should follow journalistic principles within the context of the theme or style of your paper. In other words, you will want to quote sources. But you don't have to use "dry" language.

- A personal statement, which can read like a letter to the reader or an editorial. This can be about how you feel about yourself in school so far, in journalism class, in your social life, in your family, etc. This statement will probably also define the theme or overall approach of your Zine.

- A review of some kind, much like the reviews we have already done.

- Artwork throughout, with even one or two whole pages devoted to art. This can be original work of yours, something you solicit from a friend, something you borrow, a collage, some photography, etc. Don't make it boring clip-art off the computer. One requirement: There should be at least one photo of you in the Zine.

You may choose to type some of the Zine's copy and handwrite some of it. You might get a friend with good calligraphy skills to copy one of the articles. Of course, all the work can be written up on other paper, then cut and glued onto your Zine paper. Then you photocopy it to get a clean copy. And, yes, you can color-copy certain pages if you want color to come through.

We will be sharing the progress of your Zine on _____(dates)_____. On each of these days you must have at least one article to share with the class, to show your progress. You must have the final, final version on _____(date)_____.

Rubric for Grading of Zine (total points: 120)

Use the following rubric as a guide when you are working on your Zine. The rubric should help you think about how to prioritize the work.

	FULL POINTS	PARTIAL POINTS	NO POINTS
NEWS ARTICLE	*20 points:* Well-researched, uses quotations, observes journalistic principles.	*10 points:* Story with faulty premise, weakly researched, not enough quotations.	*0 points:* False or fictional story, no story, no quotes.
PERSONAL STATEMENT	*20 points:* Honest and heart-felt, thoughtful and interesting.	*10 points:* Halfhearted and vague.	*0 points:* Fake or too short or nonexistent.
REVIEW	*20 points:* Interesting, engaging, original, using detail and examples.	*10 points:* Falls victim to cliché, gives opinion without context.	*0 points:* Flat and boring, too short.
ARTWORK	*20 points:* Creative, original, thoughtful both on art page and throughout Zine.	*10 points:* Creative work but minimal, limited to art page.	*0 points:* Crude, whipped out in a few minutes.
CREATIVITY	*20 points:* Zine represents you, makes the reader laugh, think, reflect.	*10 points:* Zine has some good ideas but is uneven.	*0 points:* Zine is not thought out, not coherent.
PROMPTNESS	*20 points:* You have something to share both Fridays, and you hand it in at the beginning of class on the due date.	*10 points:* You are late on one Friday but also share with class your work in progress and are on time on the due date.	*0 points:* You are late, late, and late again.

Zine Grading Rubric

	POINTS
NEWS ARTICLE	
PERSONAL STATEMENT	
REVIEW	
ARTWORK	
CREATIVITY	
PROMPTNESS	

Zine Grading Rubric

	POINTS
NEWS ARTICLE	
PERSONAL STATEMENT	
REVIEW	
ARTWORK	
CREATIVITY	
PROMPTNESS	

Zine Grading Rubric

	POINTS
NEWS ARTICLE	
PERSONAL STATEMENT	
REVIEW	
ARTWORK	
CREATIVITY	
PROMPTNESS	

Zine Grading Rubric

	POINTS
NEWS ARTICLE	
PERSONAL STATEMENT	
REVIEW	
ARTWORK	
CREATIVITY	
PROMPTNESS	

Book Three: Cleaning Up; Watching

DISCUSSION QUESTIONS

Terkel says in his introduction (p. xxi) that "More people are being paid to watch other people than ever before. A cargo inspector says, 'I watch the watchman.' " Why is there so much security and watching in our society? Do we have more or less "watching" today?

What do you know about the custodian at your school? About the security people?

What myths, positive and negative, do you ascribe to the police? What new information did you gain from reading the interviews with Vincent Maher and Renault Robinson (pp. 129–143)? What do you think Mr. Robinson would say about the Rodney King incident, when police in Los Angeles were captured on videotape brutally beating a suspect they had stopped?

ACTIVITIES

Terkel talks in the introduction about John R. Coleman, the president of Haverford College, taking an experiential sabbatical—during which he worked menial jobs, got fired, was unemployed. While now we have "Take Your Daughter to Work Day," students seldom get a chance to go and find out what others' lives are like, especially those on the bottom of society.

But students *can* go beyond interviewing. They can shadow their subjects, or become a participant/observer. The Diversity Project—a research and reform partnership between Berkeley High School and the University of California at Berkeley—enlisted teachers and U.C. graduate students to conduct extensive interviews with sixteen high school juniors. Then they shadowed each student for a day, going to each class and lunch, observing the teaching as well as the social life the student experienced. For the shadowers, the day became much like it was for the students, an exercise in endurance as the clock ticked off through each class.

I was once a legal observer for a homeless encampment, and for four nights I slept outside in the park. The experience led to an awareness I would never have had through all the discussions of homelessness. I realized the obvious point that we choose to forget in inuring ourselves to those begging on every block: that no one chooses to be homeless; no one in the middle of the night, with rats crawling over them, with cold and dew and dirt, thinks this is just a lifestyle choice. So I challenged my students once, when they were deciding who to talk to for their interview project, to consider being homeless for a day. There were dangers, of course, though not great. But I insisted they only do this with parental permission.

To my surprise, two students took me up on the challenge. They were homeless for a scant 14 hours, but it became one of the major experiences of their high school careers for both of them. Here is the account of one of these students:

Being Homeless: A First-Hand Experience

"I'll be fine, Mom, don't worry," I told my mom as I informed her of my plan to be homeless for a night. She didn't like the idea one bit and wasn't hesitating to tell me so. My dad wasn't any different. It didn't change my parents' minds when I said that if anything came up I would call them (something homeless people can't do). Luckily, in the end my mom allowed me to make my own decision. I decided to be homeless. I knew that after this experience I would have learned more than I could have from reading books and asking questions.

The next day I went to school with a mat and a backpack

full of ratty clothes. When students found out about my activity they looked at me crazily. They couldn't comprehend why I would do such a thing. "It's only Journalism 1," they would say. But I knew it wasn't "only Journalism 1." My experience would allow me to have a different perspective, one that I couldn't have from the comfort of my home.

Technically I was "homeless" after school. I now had no home so I couldn't go home. I just hung out. I ended up waiting for Avery, my partner on this assignment, in a back alley, under some stairs, while he tried to convince his parents that being homeless for a night wouldn't be so bad. After waiting for what seemed a very long time, Avery came back. He had gotten the okay.

Right away I experienced a downside of being homeless— one has to carry all his belongings with him. I had a backpack, a mat, and a sleeping bag. The same was true for Avery. In the end we ended up strapping our mats and sleeping bags to our backpacks. Because our clothes weren't dirty, ripped or stained, we ended up looking more like a couple of trekkers rather than a couple of homeless kids.

The looks and stares began when we got up to Shattuck and University. I noticed that we were never asked for "spare change" anymore. It was beginning to get dark so we decided to "hit Telly (Telegraph) for dinner."

We only had enough money for a couple of drinks and a half a slice of pizza for each of us. After buying some drinks, we went price shopping for a slice of pizza. At $2.50 a slice La Val's was out of our price range. Blondie's was much more reasonable at $2.25. We ordered a cheese and pineapple slice and split it up between the two of us. I devoured my half quickly and was left with a desire for more but our budget now consisted of $0.08.

By now it was dark and beginning to rain. Our priority was to find a dry shelter where we could spend the night. We walked around some and finally found an empty church being remodeled on Frat Row. It seemed safe so we chose it to be where we were going to sleep.

We laid our sleeping bags out around 10:15 P.M. and tried to go to sleep. I say tried because I never was able to go fully to sleep. Many students from Cal walked right past us and most were loud and boisterous (probably drunk). Then around 1:00 A.M. some homeless guy woke both Avery and me up.

"Hey, man, can I sleep with you guys?" he asked. I wasn't sure if I was having a bad dream so I ignored him.

"Yo, is it cool if I sleep with you guys? . . . Guys?"

Finally Avery, after staring directly at him for a couple minutes, said, "Yeah, it's cool."

We ended up talking with this guy before going back to sleep and found out his name was Steve. He told us he was from Seattle and then he asked us where we were from.

"Oh . . . we're from the other side of town," Avery said, trying to sound as homeless as possible.

I then tried to go to sleep. I wasn't able to. It wasn't because I was cold. It wasn't because I thought Steve from Seattle might be up to something, nor was it because we were hassled by residents. I just couldn't go to sleep.

Steve woke us up at 6:30 A.M.

"Hey man, you got the time?" he asked.

"Six-thirty," I replied.

"Thanks, man."

Steve then told us his plans for the day. "Yeah, I'm going down to Sutter and Telegraph to get some breakfast, then I'm meeting up with some friends and going to San Fran. I got to pick up my welfare check and get to the marijuana club."

"That's cool," said Avery as if he had been there and done that.

"Yeah man, it looks like you guys will be fine. You have good (sleeping) bags and gear."

And then Steve left.

By now being homeless was taking its toll. I was tired, I hadn't brushed my teeth and was not caring about my appearance. What I cared about was getting breakfast.

After talking with Avery we decided a good meal would suit us well. Unfortunately we only had $0.08. So we decided our homeless experience should be concluded. We called up a friend and he gave us a ride back to Avery's house. There we dropped off our sleeping bags, got money and went to eat breakfast. We were no longer homeless. When we went to eat breakfast I was asked if I had any "spare change." I gave the guy $0.95 because I understood what he was going through.

Have students experience being homeless, if only for one day without the overnight. Or have them spend a day with the person they are interviewing, shadowing him/her at work or at school. This can be written up in conjunction with an interview.

Have students develop a project to investigate the world of work today, including job options in the new economics compared with those in the 1970s. A core issue should be about work and satisfaction. How do we see making the world a better place? Have students look at the section in *Working* by Pauline Kael, pp. 155–156, and read aloud the footnote at the bottom of page 156. Ask what this suggests about the power of advertising. Read aloud the interview with photographer Jill Freedman, pp. 153–154. Have students write a reflective paper about work and satisfaction, or about school and satisfaction.

Book Four: The Demon Lover: The Making; The Driving; The Parking; The Selling

DISCUSSION QUESTIONS

Discuss how automobiles affect the lives of Americans. How are automobiles a metaphor for our time? Under what conditions are automobiles produced in Korea, Japan, Mexico?

Auto accidents are still the leading cause of teenage deaths. What is the allure of the car for teens? Can this ever change? How will people be transported in 100 years?

What is the difference in the point of view of the factory worker and that of the foreman or manager?

ACTIVITIES

This section suggests all kinds of activities using the automobile as the organizing principle. Terkel says in the introduction (p. xxi): "An unusually long sequence of this book is devoted to the automobile—its making, its driving, its parking, its selling. Also its servicing. There is its residue, too: traffic, noise, accident, crime, pollution, TV commercials, and human orneriness at its worst."

Students can conduct interviews to update this section, organizing an oral history investigation around the automobile or some other artifact of our society.

Students can also make a journalism assignment out of this section, doing a feature story on automobiles in the school parking lot, with a photo spread and interviews with car owners.

Revisit the discussion in the previous section about the play produced on the top floor of a large parking garage in which the actors all sat in automobiles, talking with friends, lovers, and family members, and the audience walked around among the automobiles, listening to dialogue, watching the interactions. Ask students to create their own version of this drama. (See Drama lesson plan, p. 66.)

Have students research the changing economy and the drop in automobile manufacturing in the United States. Students should be cautioned not to fall into the American exceptionalism mistake, imagining that somehow industrial labor is gone from the world entirely and we have entered an "information age." The change mostly means that industrial labor has moved out to poorer countries around the world. Help students investigate: What are the factory conditions in other parts of the world? What are the tensions and contradictions?

Have students write a series of letters to automobile manufacturers, dealerships, and advertising agencies. Ask for their views on the importance of the automobile today. Then have them compare and contrast the responses with interviews they conduct with other people in this field.

At Berkeley High School, teachers Bill Pratt and Frank Schooley coordinate the BEST program, which stands for Berkeley Experiential Student Transition. Seniors spend their spring semester pursuing their own projects, investigating possible career fields, creative projects, internships, and community service. They use *Working* as the common text, the opportunity for students to come together to read about lives in work. Students write in journals about their experiences and create essays that compare their experiences to those in the book.

Book Five: Appearance; Counting; Footwork; Just a Housewife

DISCUSSION QUESTIONS

How much money is spent every year on cosmetics and beauty supplies? What is the standard of beauty in our society?

Where do banks make their profits? How is the banking industry changing today?

What kinds of tensions do people encounter in jobs with public contact, whether it is as an elevator operator, waitress, or supermarket checker?

There is a great mystique and mythology around waitressing jobs. Have students name some movies and books with this occupation. Why is this job often used as a metaphor?

What kinds of jobs are more often women's jobs? How is women's work valued? One activist group is called Wages for Housework. What do you suppose the platform of this group is?

Sometimes Studs Terkel organizes sections around common jobs; other times there is something strange and quirky about the grouping of people. What do you suppose is the organizing principle of "Footwork"?

Jesusita Novarro says (p. 305), "People say, I'm down. I'll stay down. And this goes on generation to generation to generation. Their daughter and their daughter and their daughter. . . . These kids don't ask to be born—these kids are gonna grow up and give their lives one day. There will always be a Vietnam. There will always be war." Do you agree with this? Why or why not? What actions of human beings are the result of "human nature" and what are learned by people because of the historical period they live in?

ACTIVITY

This is a section that brings up issues of gender and power in our society. After reading "Appearance," pursue a unit on body image in our society. Have students bring in magazine clippings of models and famous people. Track the number of photographs of women in the *New York Times* and describe what they look like. This can be done only through tracking news and feature text. Or you could include advertisements, which opens up new areas of discussion. One student of mine found that the women were either anorexic models or motherly older women. Seldom were they identified for their accomplishments alone.

Pippa Norris at Harvard has done extensive work on how women are framed in the media, as either the seductress or the mother. A similar study can be done on race in the media, on the framing of the gay subjects, even on certain professions.

Many authors have paid homage to Studs Terkel in their own work gathering stories. Sydney Lewis is a Chicago author who started out working for Terkel and soon became his friend and an oral historian in her own right. She created *Hospital: An Oral History of Cook County Hospital* and a profile of teenagers from their own perspective in *A Totally Alien Life Form*. The latter is particularly fascinating for students because the organizing principle is not work but being a teen, something they know plenty about. Here's how history teacher Meredith McMonigle uses it at Berkeley High:

> We picked a story that is accessible and short, like the first one, with Annie Garcias. Students discussed it together, outlining the big topics, what issues she covers, such as emigration, family, school, etc. I wrote this on the board as we are talking.
>
> Then the class brainstormed what questions they thought Sydney Lewis asked in order to get this monologue. Since she edits out the question, just as Studs Terkel does, we tried to figure out her side of the conversation. We then discussed, what would some other good questions be?

Students then paired up—I chose the partners based on students I wanted to get to know each other—to interview each other in class. I told them to take notes, try to get a flavor for a person's voice, write down as much as you can. Students were then to write up their interview at home. I was surprised at how many came in with text that was very close to a transcription. Then they would put descriptions of the scene in parentheses—body language, gestures, how their partner looked, other observations.

While they were giving the reports, I took photographs of the students. Then I could put the interviews on the board, with photographs adorning them, as a display for the classroom.

We use this activity to get students interested in oral history. We can then take the experience and apply it to a local immigration study or anything else connected with our history curriculum.

Sydney Lewis's latest release is *Help Wanted: Tales from the First Job Front* (The New Press). This is a fantastic addition to *Working*—something that students can use to imagine their job futures and pursue their research on the economy and school-to-career options. The following excerpt, from T. J. Devoe in 1997, suggests the possibilities this book offers.

When T. J., eighteen, discovered music, he felt he'd found his calling. "I play drums in a band, and that's my dream, to be in music." He decided to take a semester off and earn money before entering college to pursue music studies. "I don't know anything. I can barely read music. I'm looking to learn different types of techniques so I can better myself as a musician." T. J.'s first job was at a supermarket. From the agony of being bored to the annoyance of conforming to the corporate image, "It shattered my idea of work a little bit." A mental-health facility data-entry job better suited him and increased his compassion for others. A summer house-painting stint was hard work, and he feels work at a flower store where he's currently a part-time employee is "the coolest job." Seeing a successful

*small business has given him ideas about what he might some-
day achieve. T. J. was in his first term of college when we spoke.*

When I graduated from high school I was overwhelmed. People go through high school and they get to be seniors and
they're like, I'm *huge* now. And then it's over and you've got
a whole new life. I wasn't really scared, but having this vast
range of opportunity made me uneasy. I didn't know *what* was
gonna happen. But then I took the attitude that whatever happens, what matters is what I make of it.

When I was a kid, work was the farthest thing from my
mind. I was thinking more about what it would be like going
to high school. In grade school, I got into drawing and doing
art. When I was fifteen, I found music, and that just *took* me,
I fell in love. I used to write rhymes, and I rapped with these
guys in a band. We didn't have a drummer, so I'd fill in. I
didn't know how to play: it was just stick banging and loud
noise, like what mothers hate.

I messed around with the drums a bunch, and then one
day I found out I could separate, keep different beats and
times. It's like being ambidextrous: you do two different things
with your hands.

I didn't start loving music until I found out I could be
good at it. I looked at music and thought, "I could do something with this." But it's not a perfect world, you don't always
get what you want, it's not guaranteed. I needed to think about
something a *little* more practical to fall back on. I looked at
my choices and thought, "What do I want to do? Am I serious
about music?" I had to ask myself realistic questions: What
if I'm not good enough? So I'm majoring in sound recording
and acoustics—I can work in recording studios. If I can't be
performing, I want to be close to the business. But I worried,
what if the recording thing turns out to be completely boring?

My band recorded something in a little studio last year,
and it's buttons and knobs, thousands of them. I'm going to
have to learn what every one of them does. But now that I'm
in school, I realize it's not as drab as I feared. And my attitude

is that I *have* to learn this to make the music sound good. It's for the music and that's what I love.

My mom and dad separated when I was real young. My mom's white, my dad's black, but people think I'm Mexican or Greek. I guess I don't talk like people's stereotype of a black man. My dad's been a cook in a hotel for ten years now and seems to enjoy it. My mom works at a place that has something to do with workers' unions, and also at a mental-health facility, doing stuff with client information.

I was fifteen when I got my first job. I needed money and my mom was always telling me, "Get a job"—typical parent thing. So I was like, I gotta do it, be responsible, and then I can buy things for myself. I got hired at the supermarket down the road. But I *hated* that job 'cause it was just standing around the whole time, putting food in bags. It was empty labor to me—it wasn't *doing* anything. I worked from around four until ten on school nights, and on the weekends till one in the morning. Basically, I'd punch in, stand at the register, put food in bags and give them to people. And then I'd go outside and get carts. We'd have to do that in freezing-cold weather and on blistering-hot days. People would give me attitude and expect me to be all *happy*. "Oh, here you go, here's your food, enjoy it!" And look at this job I'm doing. People wouldn't be happy if *they* were at this end.

At the orientation, you spent the whole day sitting in the lounge where employees take their breaks. You watched movies on how to be a good bagger and then you went out and you were *bagging* . . . A good bagger packs the food without crushing fragile things, like fruits and bread. Cereal boxes go on the ends, so you have room in the middle. Just little tricks. That was interesting for, like, a split second. That's pretty much *it*.

They had their whole code of *smile* and *do this, don't do that*. And the outfit! For orientation you were supposed to wear a white shirt and black jeans. I didn't know, so I went kind of casual. I wore black jeans, but I had a white shirt with little black designs. When I went into the store for training, all the other employees were looking at me like "who's *this* guy?" One of the customer-service desk people said, "Tell that kid if he wants to keep this job, he's gotta wear the right outfit." I was embarrassed, but I didn't *know*.

Plus, I had crazy hair. It was long, but shaved on the side. I'd pull it back in a ponytail for work. Some of the customers looked at me like I was this big freak. It was weird 'cause I was just trying to be myself. I thought I could be myself and still do a good job. But they wanted this corporate company image, so being uniform and conforming was like a *big* deal to them.

There were older people there, in their twenties. They were all friends and had been working at the store for five or six years. They had their own little life together outside of the store, they'd socialize. It was obnoxious,'cause they'd talk about this person or that person. You'd get tired of hearing the gossip, you wanted to hear something *else*. And I'm thinking, "How could you want to be a cashier for eight or nine hours a day and just stand there and get sore feet?" [He shakes his head in disbelief.] I quit because it was getting in the way of school and I just couldn't *stand* it.

Then I didn't work for awhile 'cause I was kind of iffy after that grocery store. After about six months, I was desperate for money. I got a job at the mental-health facility where my mom works—from the summer before my senior year all the way through that year. That job gave me a better outlook. My mom had worked there for fifteen, sixteen years, so everyone knew about me and they were real nice people. The only downside was that *everyone* knew about me—I felt like I had to live up to this image. People heard stories from my mom, "Oh, he's in art, he's in music," and then I would come in and would be like, "Here I am." It seemed to confuse people. They expected this huge vibrant personality, you know, and I don't talk that much, I kind of keep to myself.

The job was doing data entry—I learned how to type in school. Most of the time I was alone in a room. Sometimes I like to work by myself because then I don't feel I have to work *and* provide conversation, I can get down to business. I entered information about clients, their names and where they lived, and sometimes information about why they were in the mental-health facility—like if they had drug problems or were schizophrenic.

I'd look at people on the street and wonder what kind of problems they might have. Are they mentally healthy? You don't usually think about that. You get an idea that everyone's OK from the people you deal with, and from what you see on TV. You start thinking people who *do* have problems are just scummy and evil. But there are *so many* people with problems. I liked that the job gave me a different view. I'm a good listener, and when something's bothering someone I try and help. That job made me want to help people more.

The summer after high school, I took a house-painting job with someone in my band. I took it for the experience and to do something different. We painted for a national franchise that hires college students. We woke up every morning around six o'clock and went to job sites and worked on houses all day. At first I didn't like it 'cause of the routine. That was probably the most strenuous job I ever had. I'd come home with paint all over me, every day, sore feet, *dead* tired. But then I got into it and was like, "You gotta wake up every morning, you have to do this, stop complaining and *do* it."

My manager was really strict. You weren't allowed to get paint droplets *anywhere*. When you scraped paint, everything had to be clean, otherwise you'd have to do it over again, and spend extra hours cleaning what you messed up. We worked on a time budget. If you didn't get the house painted in a certain amount of time, you'd have to work on it without getting paid. It made you hustle. You had to maintain a constant speed, you had to pace yourself. [He claps rapidly.]

I enjoyed being outside all day . . . in good weather. Being with my friend, listening to music while we worked. Old people brought us lemonade, pitchers of root beer, brownies. They pretty much kept to themselves, just let us do our work. But we had houses where people were really picky and they would stand outside and watch. Or, like, if we were painting a window, they'd be on the inside looking out. When people are staring at you, expecting you to do a perfect job, that makes you more prone to mess up.

I never thought house-painting could be so *interesting*. I got into all the different tools you use. You have a "five-in-one," this little scraper tool that does five different things—cleans paint rollers, scrapes paint, it's a putty knife—and you have big scrapers and rollers. We'd go to the store and look at all these paints and the way they mix them, so I got an idea of different paint textures.

I developed an extreme hatred for oil-based paint. [Smiles.] I had to paint all these iron rails with black oil paint . . . on one of the hottest days of the summer. I was a messy painter—not on the job site, but on myself. If I got paint on my hands, I would wipe it wherever. And I got this stuff *all over* me. My foreman said, "That's *oil* paint, that's not coming off for a while." I went home for lunch and showered—it didn't come off. On the hottest day of the summer, it's not great to have black on because it absorbs heat. That black paint was stuck on me for a week.

The foreman was twenty-one, and he was cool. He was on the job site all the time. As long as we kept to the time budget and got our work done, he let us take breaks, even when we weren't supposed to. But the franchise manager, he was a complete *jerk*. He only came on the job site every once in a while, to monitor our progress. When I first started, he talked to me like I was some sort of idiot. I'm painting, and he's like, "Oh, you want to do it like this and like this." And I'm like, "Well, the way I'm doing it, it still looks good." I don't always do it the textbook way, I form my own ways.

This job was full-time, five days a week. When I started, I was told we didn't have to work on the weekends. But some-times we went over budget on houses, and even when we didn't, the manager made us come in on Saturdays. The first three times I didn't say anything, but then it got to be *every* Saturday. Sometimes it would be on Sundays too . . . *NO*. I understand that I'm giving this guy my time and it's a job that has to be done. But when it's every weekend, and it's summer, and I just graduated . . . I wanted to have some fun, too. It was strenuous work and I needed a break. If you overwork people, they're not going to do as good a job.

I asked my foreman, "What's going on? I thought we got weekends off, I thought that's how it's supposed to be." And he said, "Yeah, it is." I felt like I was some kind of pawn, like *all* of us were. The manager would say, "I'm thinking about getting these houses done, I've got jobs lined up." I understood his position: he's got all these jobs lined up and he wants them done so *he* makes *his* money. He was selfish, just thinking about how everything's gonna work for him. Sometimes he scheduled budgets that were ridiculous, and those were the ones we would go over on. He wasn't thinking about our needs, or how if you want us to do a house in this little amount of time it's gonna look like *crap*.

We had this porch job—the worst job we had. Our foreman went back to school three days into the job. That left just me and my friend. We went over budget by a week. Our manager knew the foreman was leaving, he knew me and my friend were first-year painters. He should have known the job would take longer, he should have allowed more time. But he would say, "See this right here? That should take about two hours. And this over here, the soffit and the ceiling, that should take three hours." I guess he thought, "If there were two of me doing this job, we could do it in this amount of time." And I'm like, "Well, you gotta remember we're still rookies—we're not as good as you are."

An old lady lived in the basement and she would try and direct us without having any *idea* what she was talking about. It was sort of the blind leading the blind. She always called us by our names and it got to where I was sick of hearing my own name. "T. J., there's paint chips over *there*." She's an old lady, I guess you can't be too hard on her, but it was a nightmare, that porch, a big three-floor monster.

We had to paint everything: the posts, the roofs for each

level, the floors, the stairs. We made a lot of sloppy mistakes 'cause we were over budget and we weren't getting paid for *any* of this. That made it worse. Each morning I dreaded going back because we weren't doing the quality we were supposed to do, the quality we really enjoyed doing. It was just painting. [Mimes slopping paint on.] Not taking any pride at all.

That bothered me because I liked making people's houses look nice, bettering them. We had some houses that were in terrible shape—ratty paint, peeling everywhere. And when we're done, the house has a sort of glow. You can stand back and look. *I* did that masterpiece—I made that house look *great*.

After the summer, I started working at a flower shop. A friend's parents own it—his mother does the designing, his father manages the store. I got hired around Christmas because they needed extra help. I put labels on mailers and the manager showed me how to wrap and do basic things around the store. I didn't know that jobs like this existed. I always think of work as serious, but this is fun. There are days when I'm wrapping packages and doing odds and ends around the store and it doesn't feel like I'm working. It's not at all like the supermarket job. I deliver flowers to people's houses and to hospitals and places all over the area. Flowers have an effect. I deliver to people that are sick or in nursing homes, and when they see flowers coming, everyone gets all happy and cheery. Offices are the craziest, everyone loses their mind—"Oh, is that for *me?*"

I never thought you could make so much money running a flower shop. My friend's mother is a great floral designer, and that was her dream. She's always studying flowers. She has meetings with other designers across the globe—she's been to Bangkok, in Thailand, and to Japan. I never thought you could do all these great things just by running a tiny little business. I'm looking at them and how they're living: as their own bosses, doing what they want. That makes me look at *my* situation and what I want to do. It makes me think about having goals.

I'd like to be my own boss. Maybe open my own recording studio, depending on how things go with my studies and music. I could rent an apartment and have the studio right in there, soundproof it and all that. All you really need are the resources and the knowledge. It's easier to think about the recording studio than wonder, "Am I gonna make it? Am I gonna be a superstar?" Taking a more realistic view is comforting. It makes my future more definite.

I want to do something that's gonna make me happy. I don't want to spend the rest of my life thinking, "What could I have done?" I don't want to sit back and think about all the things I could've been. I want to at least *try*, I want to take the chance. So, now I see what I want to do. I'm just striving for the goal.

I think you have to know yourself, know what you want to do, and what you want for yourself in the future, and then take the steps necessary to provide that. You have to go into every new situation thinking of how you want it to work for you. Sometimes that knowledge doesn't come to you right away. You gotta experience, you gotta live, you gotta *do*.

Book Six: The Quiet Life; Brokers; Bureaucracy; Organizer

DISCUSSION QUESTIONS

On page xviii of his introduction, Terkel talks about something he learned from a comment made by a hospital aide when he interviewed her for *Division Street: America*. The idea was that you have to have a "feeling tone." This term is something that he has mulled over and over for years. What do you think it means? How does it apply to these characters? To your life?

What is the attraction of bookbinding (p. 309)? What does Donna Murray mean by "I'm just a swabber. I'm not an artist"? What about the piano tuner when he says, "I am not the slightest bit status conscious" (p. 319)?

What are the attractions and frustrations of being a broker to the wealthy?

After reading the section "Bureaucracy" (pp. 341–351), develop a profile of work in a bureaucracy. Use your own city bureaucracy or school bureaucracy as a model. How does it compare to Kafka's nightmare vision in *The Trial*? What is the way these project coordinators find satisfaction?

After reading the interview with Bill Talcott (pp. 352–356), discuss what kind of union organizing is going on today.

ACTIVITIES

Look back on the readings by Jill Freedman and Pauline Kael, (pp. 153–156) as well as the organizer interview (Bill Talcott, pp. 352–356), to open a discussion on students as change agents.

All of this forces the teacher to look to the ethical side of teaching. So much school-to-work promotion these days is about the need to create better, passive workers for the current economy. A speaker at my school enthused, "We got a group of eight CEOs together and just asked them, 'What do you need? What are you lacking in today's school graduates?' " Is this the best way to organize and plan curriculum?

The Freedman and Kael interviews push us to develop a discussion about job satisfaction and alienation, making money, and community service. Develop a project based on community service. Require each student to do 16–20 hours of something useful to the community. The students can keep journals about their experience, make oral reports to the class, or do more formal writing. This should not be just "serving food at a soup kitchen." It should be something creative and engaging that makes the world a better place. While some may complain about this assignment, it is satisfying to see the excitement they bring back after their experience. This project can of course be extended, to a senior project or group commitment to a social action or community service agency.

Movie Project

Organize a film festival at school on the subject of work. Have students research movies that have the theme of work, workplace organizing, or careers. The film festival can be held during class or after school. Students can then critique the films through their own videotaped "review," writing projects, or Socratic seminar discussions. Some titles that leap to mind are Charlie Chaplin's *Modern Times*, the Richard Pryor classic about auto-plant work, *Blue Collar*, the feminist *9 to 5* starring Lily Tomlin and Jane Fonda, Martin Ritt's *Norma Rae*, John Sayles's *Matewan*,

Mike Nichols's *Silkwood*, and Herbert Biberman's 1954 story of a farm-workers' strike, *Salt of the Earth*, made with artists all blacklisted by Hollywood after the McCarthy hearings in the 1950s.

You can also study documentaries such as Barbara Kopple's award-winning *Harlan County U.S.A.* as well as her *American Dream*, Debra Chasnoff's *Deadly Deception*, Connie Field's *The Life and Times of Rosie the Riveter*, Michael Moore's New-Journalistic *Roger and Me*, and the series *We Do the Work*. A great documentary and reflection on the economy is *Who's Counting?* by Marilyn Waring.

Classes can also explore the relationship between song and work, again through comparison with *Working*. Students can develop a collection of songs, or write and sing their own songs about labor. Sometimes here there are tie-ins with movies, such as the film *Coal Miner's Daughter*, which features the classic country songs of Loretta Lynn. There are hundreds of country and folk songs about work in the collections of Woody Guthrie (see especially "Plane Crash over Los Gatos"), U. Utah Phillips, and even Johnny Paycheck, with his modern classic anthem of working class frustration, "Take This Job and Shove It." African-American blues singer Leadbelly did dozens of work songs, including "John Henry," "Rock Island Line," and "House of the Rising Sun." Even John Lennon checks in with "Working Class Hero."

Some songs are written to be sung while working, to keep the mind occupied and to help those working together on gang projects. The call-and-response spirituals and work songs of the African-American South have their roots in slavery—roots that have been traced to group labor agricultural practices in Africa. Other songs are meant to be sung in the pub after work or in prison during protests about work. Welsh miners have massive choral groups of working men—who sing about work, life, and their struggles. Ask students how many more tunes they can find in libraries, record collections, even the memories of their grandparents. What are they saying?

Book Seven: The Sporting Life; In Charge; Ma and Pa Courage; Reflections on Idleness and Retirement

DISCUSSION QUESTIONS

How do the sporting accounts differ from the romanticized public image of athletes?

Compare the sports press agent Blackie Mason (p. 373) with stage press agent Eddie Jaffe (p. 85).

What perspective on work and making a profit do executives and managers share?

What do you learn about aging and retirement in this section? Studs Terkel has written a number of books on the elderly. As the baby-boom generation gets older, there are more movies with aged heroes, more legislation to favor older citizens. This is probably because the "boomer" generation caused a large increase in the population and came to wield a powerful force on the market—what boomers wanted, the market needed to supply. Now that the baby boomers are aging, geriatrics and the attraction of aging begin to dominate the culture.

ACTIVITIES

Have students read "The Sporting Life" section in conjunction with re-search on a sport or reading a book on sports. Some fields, like baseball, have generated hundreds of books by fans, participants, experts, and amateurs. Students can form groups based on the sport they are interested in and report on it. The activities that reflect on favorite sports can explore what is attractive and miraculous about the sport; they can also seek to rid students of illusions, like the hopes of so many high school students that they will get rich by getting to the NBA. View the video *Hoop Dreams* directed by Steve James or read all or parts of the book *Hoop Dreams* written by Ben Joravsky (1995, Turner Publishing).

Poetry Project

Terkel refers (p. xxxi) to the poem by Bertolt Brecht, "A Worker Reads History." It deals with the contradiction in work and power: owners and bosses get credit for great cities, but it is the anonymous workers who actually construct them. Find other poems that meditate on the pain and dignity of work. Carl Sandburg's "Chicago" is a classic example and one that Studs often cites. The great nineteenth-century democrat Walt Whitman wrote the classic American paean to workers and their contribution, "I Hear America Singing." Fifty years later, Harlem Renaissance poet Langston Hughes corrected and criticized Whitman's poem when he wrote "I, Too," pointing out the central role of black labor in the building of America:

I, Too
by Langston Hughes

> I, too, sing America.
>
> I am the darker brother.
>
> They send me to eat in the kitchen
>
> When company comes,
>
> But I laugh,
>
> And eat well,
>
> And grow strong.

Tomorrow,

I'll sit at the table

When company comes.

Nobody'll dare

Say to me,

"Eat in the kitchen,"

Then.

Besides,

They'll see how beautiful I am

And be ashamed—

I, too, am America.

Students can read these and other poems on work, then write their own, either talking about their own work, their parents' jobs, or just work in the community. They can do a "talk back" poem to another poem, as Hughes does to Whitman.

Art Project

Have students read a section, say, "Ma and Pa Courage," pp. 414–421, then paint or draw a picture depicting something in that story. Students can collect and study art on work. See, for instance, "Construction of the Dam" by William Gropper, a mural at the Department of the Interior in Washington, D.C., and other paintings of work done during the Depression by the Work Projects Administration (WPA) on post offices and public buildings throughout the country. Coit Tower in San Francisco has a massive mural depicting California labor.

Students can also develop a discussion on the core meaning of work based on one of the sections in the book and then go out in the world and sketch working situations.

Photography

While capturing the spoken word is a key activity students explore in response to *Working*, students can also use the book as a jumping off point for many other media—artwork, video, even photography. Here are some ideas on photography: Read and discuss the monologues by Peter Keeley and Lois Keeley Novak (pp. 401–405). Have students go out and photograph fathers and daughters. Create a classroom display. Discuss the relationships. Do the same with other relationships. Or, have students create a photo exhibit on one industry or work area in your town based on their own photos. Or do an extended photo essay on one person's workday, creating a series of 25 to 30 shots taken through the day.

Photographs can be presented with or without captions. Discuss the advantages and disadvantages of each type of presentation. A more off-beat photo assignment, but one that provokes interesting discussion and reflection, is to have students choose one character from *Working* and go out and take a photo of someone they think could be the person speaking. The look of the person, how he/she gestures, etc., should all fit with the photographer's idea of what he/she looks like. Then the class puts all the photos on the board and, after discussion, votes to choose the one that fits best.

Another photo activity, which ties in to issues in biography, is to have students bring in a series of photographs from their grandparents or great-grandparents. After looking closely at the photos, and remembering what they know of their family history, students write a detailed story, a remembrance, about the family. For prompts on how to look at a photograph and make deductions and speculations, see a number of photo poems by Sharon Olds: "Photograph of the Girl," "Nevsky Prospekt (July, 1917)," and "I Go Back to May, 1937."

Book Eight: The Age of Charlie Blossom; Cradle to the Grave

DISCUSSION QUESTIONS

Why does Studs Terkel call this section "The Age of Charlie Blossom"? How does Charlie's experience stand for the experience of his generation? What do you think Charlie is doing today?

Imagine a debate between Charlie Blossom (p. 437) and Ralph Werner (p. 452). How would each describe the other?

What different educational philosophies are displayed by the public school teacher and the alternative school teacher? How does your school compare to these two types of schools and teachers?

How do the experiences of the hospital aide and the patients' representative compare to the images of hospitals presented in popular television shows such as *ER* and *Chicago Hope*?

ACTIVITIES
Thanatopsis Project

Young people have a fascination with death. I've known seven-year-olds who want to investigate death, visit a graveyard, read about and discuss it. In high school and college, death holds a similar fascination. Sometimes this does not suggest that students want to pursue the most profound meditation on the existential reality of death; rather, it is a desire to look into something that is an important experience about which our society maintains a hushed quiet. After reading Herbert Bach and Elmer Ruiz (pp. 505–510) in *Working,* have students do a study on death, including interviews with cemetery employees, hospice workers, the clergy, a coroner, a suicide counselor, a member of the (pro-suicide) Hemlock Society. Have them read The *American Way of Death* by Jessica Mitford. Students could even choose fiction which contemplates death, from *Macbeth* to James Agee's *Death in the Family* to Evelyn Waugh's *The Loved One* to Anne Rice's *Interview with the Vampire*. The project can include presentations ranging from discussion to posters, class books, wall displays, and videos. Note: Make sure that school authorities and parents sign off on this project before launching it.

Many authors use the power of the word to declare "I was there, I saw this, it was real." Testimonial writing is a form of empowerment, of protest, and of indictment of social injustices. Besides first-person narratives, testimonial writing can take the form of interviews, often presented as direct first-person narratives the way Terkel does. One of the main literary themes that has come out of Latin America in the twentieth century is the writing of testimonials. Read sections of *Massacre in Mexico* by Elena Poniatowska as an example of this type of writing. Have students create a study through oral history interviews that blends the Latin American testimonial style with Studs Terkel's. They can consider interviewing immigrants from Latin America, or look at some of the areas explored in Book Eight—for example, teachers or hospital workers. See also *Hospital: An Oral History of Cook County Hospital,* by Sydney Lewis (New York: The New Press, 1994).

Castes and Jobs

Have students investigate strict castes that have developed in various cultures in relation to jobs. In medieval Europe, only the Jews were allowed to lend money and charge interest and this became the reason for many anti-Jewish outbursts, especially when princes went into debt. Today in Ireland, the Tinkers are a distinct outcast group, similar to Gypsies but racially no different from other Irish. They live in camps and make minor repairs. In India, there are low castes, the "untouchables," who are restricted to certain jobs. In Japan, a lower caste group is known as the *burakumin*; they are the only ones who work with animal products, such as tanning. Ask: Are there particular castes who do particular jobs in the U.S.? Is there strict status attached to one job or another?

Students can also create a study of work and race, answering such questions as: What kinds of jobs have been open to one race or another? Is this changing? Have them explore this theme, using statistical and historical data as well as interviews. For powerful teaching materials on race and ethics, history and responsibility, see *Facing History and Ourselves, Holocaust and Human Behavior* (Brookline, MA: Facing History and Ourselves National Foundation, 1994). This is a resource book but also contains contacts for regional curriculum support people.

Book Nine: The Quiz Kid and the Carpenter; In Search of a Calling; Second Chance; Fathers and Sons

DISCUSSION QUESTIONS

Studs Terkel has a plan in the way he organizes his book. Look back at the three opening prefaces. What was the theme he wanted to start the reader out with? What does he mean by ending the book with Tom Patrick?

Many of these stories are about people in transition. Fifty years ago, people took one job and usually stayed with it their whole lives. Today, most people have three or four careers before they are done. Why has this changed?

What are the implications of generational change in the series of stories of fathers and sons? How would a comparison of mothers and daughters read differently?

ACTIVITIES

Alienation. The final book of Studs Terkel's *Working* shows people in transition, changing jobs, searching for meaning, struggling for a place in the world. Read this book carefully as a class. It circles back to a theme he introduces in the beginning, that the book is about violence and the search for daily meaning as well as bread.

As a project in cultural study, have the class investigate the issues of alienation and work. One of the classic studies of this topic in the 1950s was *Growing Up Absurd* by Paul Goodman. It explained and anticipated many of the complaints about alienation that would help define the protests of the '60s. Have the class read all or parts of this book. Another fine resource on youth and alienation is "The Port Huron Statement," the founding document found in many anthologies, of Students for a Democratic Society in the 1960s. Look also into Karl Marx's explanation of alienation, that the worker is fundamentally alienated from the product he/she makes in mass production because there is no personal relationship to it. This alienation in work is tied to a sense of disorientation, disempowerment, dissatisfaction. Find where Marx writes about this and read work of later Marxists—for example, Antonio Gramsci—on this issue. Do the same with Freud, who discusses alienation and the human condition in such works as *Civilization and Its Discontents*. This can lead to research papers, class presentations, even video presentations.

Why does Terkel speak of violence? Does he mean work is so frustrating that people break out in violence, like the cliché about the postal worker attacking his boss? Or does he mean a daily violence in the way people are treated, in the alienation they experience? Have students investigate, discuss, write about violence and work.

Discuss ethics and the development of values in the raising of children. What kinds of ethics do the workers in this section espouse? Have students read the introduction to *A Call to Character*, edited by Colin Greer and Herb Kohl, and ask: What ethical issues do we need to incorporate into the workplace? Into schools? Contact Facing History and Ourselves (16 Hurd Road, Brookline, MA 02146; 617-232-1595) for fantastic curriculum resource material on the Holocaust and on the teaching of ethics, values, and social responsibility.

Considering the search for meaning in work, have students do a family oral history of work, looking into the occupations family members have had and the significance of these jobs. Have students investigate career paths they might want to take and interview people who have jobs they aspire to.

Consider creating a radio show on work. This can be done in class with simply a tape recorder. You might be able to obtain time on a local community radio station willing to air youth viewpoints. In either case, make the show a study of work, with tapes created through interviews in the community and rolled in to live discussions. There should be a host of the show who introduces it, a discussion with the interviewers and interviewees, presentation of data or insights on work by experts, and other guests. You might include a labor organizer, a job counselor, and an industrial relations or personnel manager.

Oral history and interviewing projects can be developed with young children as well. Older students can teach younger students how to conduct interviews and help them develop oral history projects. They can interview parents and family or other interesting people in the community. Alistair Ross of London, England defines (in the journal *Oral History*, reprinted in *The Oral History Reader*) some of the advantages of conducting such a project with children aged seven to ten. These are good pedagogical goals for any interview and oral history project. He writes:

We hoped our program would develop:

- children's oral skills, of listening, questioning, talking, discussing, and arguing. These skills sometimes seem to be undervalued by parents and teachers, and need as much attention as the more formal language skills of reading and writing, if children are to be fluent communicators;
- social skills of interaction, discussion, and cooperation;
- intellectual concepts of social change, tradition, conflict, and cause;
- skills of empathy with individuals of a different generation;
- intellectual skills of sifting and selecting evidence, and making informed decisions about editing their sources;
- understanding of the problems and values of historical evidence, in particular, problems of bias and contradictory evidence;
- ability to make records and narrative accounts of what has been found.

Working with *Working* is rewarding because the text itself is so rich, the perspectives so diverse, the activities suggested so varied. In writing

Working, Studs Terkel has taken the authority to explain society out of the hands of the "experts"—the sociologists, analysts, and professors— and put it in the hands of the people to explain themselves. Likewise, bringing *Working* into the classroom centers the educational projects on the students themselves and demands that they investigate, analyze, and explain their world. This is why projects with *Working* are among the most memorable in the students' education.

III

A CONVERSATION WITH STUDS TERKEL

The Interview
(Conducted by John Ayers,
January 20, 1999)

When I first pulled up at the North Chicago brick house, a warm summer rain was starting to come down. My brother John had conducted the interview with Studs six months earlier but it had taken this long for me to get it transcribed, edit it for the first round, and get back to Chicago. Now I hoped he'd have time to take a look at the interview and give me some feedback.

I ran up to the porch and approached the door. A sign said, "Ring the bell, twice." I rang and waited. I rang again. I could hear the bell. But no one came. I wandered to the window, peeked in. A comfortable sitting room, filled with plants and books. But no answer. I rang again and again, until I heard a high-pitched woman's voice, Ida's. "Who's there?" it trilled.

"It's me, Rick."

"Oh, hi, Rick." She smiled through the door. "Just a minute." And she laboriously released the deadbolt and the large door swung back of its own weight, almost pulling her frail body over. She stood there—angelic and diminutive, no more than five feet tall—smiling up at me full face. "Just come in, Rick. I'll get him." Then she turned to the stairs and shouted loud, "Louis! Louis, Rick's here!" I knew Louis was Studs's real name but I'd never heard anyone call him that.

Studs shouted down, "Rick, is that you? I'll be right down." He soon hustled into the room, smiling full face, looking hale and hearty for his eighty-seven years. "Hey, Rick, how ya doin'? You look wonderful. How is that teaching going? Where is it, Berkeley High? What are you guys doin' out there? Wait a minute, I have to fix my ears, here. I'm deaf, you know, well, not deaf but I have to keep these hearing aids in. Only I can't put it in when stuff is flowing out. I have this infection. I always have to drain my ears. My ears—my doctor says they attract every culture that comes along. That's great, I told him, I guess they're multicultural!"

We talked and joked. As always in the presence of Studs Terkel, I felt 100 percent welcomed. I felt that the complete focus and enthusiasm and interest of the man was on me. And Ida was making that same connection. We all sat down. I commented on the beautiful display of plants at the front of the room. She beamed.

I began to explain again about the book. Studs interjected, "Oh, they're going to make a teaching guide, huh? Ideas for the classroom. I know that book, Working, *gets used for a lot of different classes." I pulled out a manuscript. Ida took the introduction and began to read. I showed Studs the interview.*

He leaned over and began reading it aloud. He would laugh and gesture as it went along, remembering a story he told, putting together the lessons learned. But he kept stopping, pointing out parts that should be changed, clarified, cleaned up. For a few pages, he would give the manuscript to me, have me make the changes. Soon, though, he had pulled out his pen and taken the draft, cradling it on his lap.

Now he was in gear, working at what he is great at, editing. Suddenly the room dropped away. Time did not matter. He was reading paragraphs out loud, mulling them over, then crossing out and adding words. He worked fast, a professional. And he dug through some of the most confusing writing, a transcript of an interview with all its hesitations, restatements, half-sentences. He looked up and smiled. "I gotta cross a lot of stuff out. It's not only repetitive, but confusing."

Sometimes he'd take something out and then decide to keep it. He wrote the journalist note, "stet," on the page so I'd know to ignore the change there. He said a few times, "You can go through and fix the tense, see, it jumps back and forth from past to present and back."

Now I would look at the pages as he turned them over and they were covered with ink. I realized that I was in the presence of the Studs Terkel creative process, the power of editing. I had always known him as the talker, the questioner, the consummate social being. But this was the first time I'd seen him edit and it dawned on me again what a dedicated practitioner he is. Now he was demonstrating his process while editing an interview with himself which explores his process.

The time flew by. It was a long manuscript, 21 pages. Ida went off to the kitchen, to get ready for a shopping expedition they had planned for later in the morning. Studs kept saying, "We're almost done. I know we have to get going." But he stopped and worked on each paragraph. He seemed worried that it would not come out right.

I wondered if I had done a terrible job of the first edit, since he was making so many changes. And indeed, he said at one point, "This should have been edited more before I saw it." That was the closest I got to a negative comment from Studs. But he was not getting personal, he was just hunched over his work. At one point he remarked: "You can make out what I'm writing here, right? I'm not getting everything. That's OK, André will see it anyway." Here he was referring to André Schiffrin, his long-time editor who was now with The New Press. The sense of respect, of collaboration, that goes into his books became clear to me.

As I sat next to him, watching him edit and stop to talk about each point, I realized again that Studs is a unique treasure of our culture, a special character created by Chicago at the second half of the century. He always got along by just being himself, by being honest and curious and ethical. Yes, ethical. Because Studs Terkel is a man on a mission. His work is not just about a method, about a way of gathering information. Such an approach, often adopted by oral historians, seems contentless and bloodless. Studs Terkel is in a struggle to create community, to discover and elevate the human soul. In spite of his casual manner of speaking, he is an intellectual and an artist. His oral history process, his way of bringing forward the core of a person, evolved from his determination to connect with people and to make us connect with each other.

He sat there for hours, muttering to himself, "No that does not make sense, let's say it this way." "Yeah, remember that guy?" Just wholly absorbed in the work at hand. And the work was in making community. And I was sitting there watching him do it.

Finally we came to the end. He held it up in triumph. "Hey! We did it, didn't we!" Always generous, always eager to share the credit. But it was his story, his mission.

I offered to drive them to the market where they were planning to shop.

"Let me run upstairs and work on my ear here, and I've gotta see a man about a dog. Then we'll go over there." I wandered around the front room, looking at the artwork, the books, the plants. What a warm and inviting home. As we left the house, he continued to enthuse, "Now, be sure to say hello to John, it's been great to see him lately. And to your father. And Bill, how's he doing? He's going to stay in Chicago, right? And what the hell's going on out there at KPFA? And your kids, I'm sure Lewis and Clark will be great for your daughter, and. . . ."

How These Oral Histories Got Started

One of the points of *Working* is that jobs are not big enough for people. That's a phrase I used. The jobs are too small for the human spirit. The nature of work. How I came to write it was André Schiffrin's idea.

A word about André Schiffrin, he's the only publisher. Except for a book I did years ago called *Times of Jazz*. That was way back, 1957. But since then all these, what are called oral histories, are under the aegis of André Schiffrin, who was with Pantheon Books that was part of Random House.

When the billionaire Newhouse took over, then books were like detergents or deodorants, what they sell. It doesn't matter, good or bad. And he was forced out because his books were very special. They didn't move fast enough. That was a big scandal in the publishing world. So he formed his own nonprofit group and I went with him. And now it's called The New Press. And he's the one who first got me to do this, way back when.

It was the sixties, Martin Luther King. The triple revolution, it was called. You know, it was the revolution in civil rights, in cybernetics, in automation. And he published the American printing of this new book about China by Jan Myrdal, the son of Gunnar Myrdal, the one who wrote *The American Dilemma*. It's called *Report from a Chinese Village*, a book about a small town in China and how that town changed as a result of the revolution, what happened to the people there, how women no longer wore tight shoes, they had unbound feet.

And it led to the idea—why not a book about an American village, Chicago, in the middle of what's happening now, revolution. So I said to him, "Are you out of your mind?" But he speaks very softly, with a British accent. He said, "Why don't you try that?" I said, "You're crazy," but I did *Division Street: America*, ordinary people's lives in a large city. And that seemed to go over well.

And then one day he said, "What about a book about the Great Depression? We ought to do that." I said, "Are you out of your mind?" And he said, "Well, let's do that." So we did *Hard Times*, which, of course, Rick and Bill and your father were in, under the name of Baird. Arthur Miller liked that book so much, he said the two great events—the two most traumatic, dramatic events in American history—were the Civil War and the Great Depression.

And as a result, his plays have always been dealing with one aspect of that Depression, of the complexity of the relationship between fathers and sons. *All My Sons* was a great one. Now, he adapted *Working* as a play. He called it *The American Clock*. He says it was inspired by *Working*. And quite a lot of the dialogue from *Working* is in the play. He has a family as the key thing. But *The American Clock* was inspired, he said, by *Working*. It still is around.

There's now a musical of *Working*. The story behind the musical is very interesting. A guy named Stephen Schwartz did it. And he wanted to make a musical. He's the one who did *Pippin* and *Godspell*.

He and others wrote the songs, himself, James Taylor, Micki Grant, Craig Cornelia. But it was overdone. It was overproduced. And so it flopped on Broadway. But since then hundreds of performances, in colleges, in high schools, in communities have done it, simply, and it has a very great track record. And the simpler, the better.

So that's the book. Now, the reason, I suppose, that the book has caught on is because of what Freud said in *Civilization and Discontents*. It's not fashionable to quote Freud these days. Freud spoke of the two prime impulses of the human being—love and work. *Liebe und arbeit*. Love and work. Love meaning sex, of course. But I think there are an awful lot of books written about sex. Probably more than we need. But hardly anything is written about work. And so that was more or less the impulse that led to it.

How can you describe man without describing how he survives? In medieval days or ancient days or prehistoric days, man was a hunter, was a fisherman. Man did something. He was a mason, was a carpenter, a farmer. He did all these, that was the nature of work. And then came the Industrial Revolution. William Blake spoke of the dark satanic mills. And then there was the effect of that, and mass production, and Henry Ford, and factories. And the whole nature of work itself took on a whole new dimension. You introduce the machine, of course. So you get man and the machine. That became part of it.

A Metaphor for Work

The section on the automobile was a big one. I called that the Demon Lover. There's an old ballad collected by Francis Child, a Harvard guy, a collector of early English ballads. One of the ballads he collected was the "Demon Lover." The demon lover is a Bluebeard, a Dracula, sort of. The demon lover's one who seduces and then kills. Now, think of the demon lover, the automobile.

Think of the automobile, what it does. How many murders are committed? Shoot, drive and shoot, shoot and drive-bys. Parking. What happens to a person inside a car? They kill for parking places. They have arguments going on all the time. There's the pollution—God knows what's happening to L.A., to Mexico City, of course, and all cities. What happens to the nerves driving the car? But, you see, man in the car feels disjointed.

Frank Lloyd Wright had a phrase. "Organic" was the key word. His architecture is organic. That is, these fingers of my hands are organic to the palm of the hand. The branches of a tree are organic to the trunk, and the trunk is organic to the ground. So when he built the Imperial Hotel in Japan, in Tokyo, there was an earthquake, a terrible earthquake, in 1924. It destroyed everything except the Imperial Hotel, because it was organic. It was connected to what he felt was the Japanese terrain. So it went along with whatever the winds were, whatever the howling blizzards were. It withstood it because it was organic.

Now, the automobile is antiorganic. You are removed. The branches are removed from the trunk but you're sitting in this car, a machine, away from everyone, so you're alone. You have a companion here and here, but you're alone. And who is the one driving the other car? He's your antagonist. He would pass by anyone, by God. We have stop lights but, generally speaking, you are out to beat the other.

Of course. That's the other thing, see? It's about the dangers of it. Now, think of the people involved in the making of an automobile. The working class, the assembly line. Then you've got the branch manager who's representing the company. Then you've got advertising. Then you've got models. Then you've got the interstate truck driver. What happens to him, you see? They're also connected with it. So what is it like to be that other person? That's the theme in all my books. What is it like to be in the position of that person, that small boy during the Great Depression? His father comes home with a tool chest on his shoulder at two o'clock in the afternoon. What happens then to that family? What was it like? And so, *Working*.

What is it like to be the salesman selling the car? Who was the one to make the car? One guy says, "Jeez, I made that, you know." And one guy would work on the assembly line, all his years, so he also becomes machine-like. He gets up and he's rushing to work. "Where are you going?" his wife says. "It's Sunday morning." "Oh, God, I'm going back to sleep."

Now, we use the automobile—that's a good metaphor to choose for this idea of work. Here you have guys in car ads—guys look at a car as if it were a woman. During one of these TV commercials during a football game you have the cars, and the guy—"Isn't she a beauty?" "Oh, wow! Look at those curves." And then you say, "This is something of a fetish. This is Krafft-Ebing. The man's fucking his car." This is interesting, isn't it? You see?

I want to tell you about this one guy, a utility guy, driving a car. It shows you about the noncelebrated, or the so-called nonintellectual, whatever phrase you want. This guy's a utility driver [Hobart Foote, p. 168] in Hammond, Indiana, part of an assembly plant there. He lives in a trailer, raises his family there. He umpires Little League games. He goes to church. He's also a witty guy, and he's got dry humor. I said, "Tell me, what's your day like? Start from the beginning." "Well, first thing, that radio goes off on the clock, and the first thing I say is, 'Oh, sheeet.' That's the first thing I say. But I open my one eye. I kiss my wife. That's routine, you understand. Then I get up and I go into the bathroom, I comb my one hair, and I sit down, and I have a cup of coffee. It may be half a cup of coffee some days, I have a toast, maybe two pieces of toast. It all depends. Then I get in the car, and my wife gives me that brown paper bag, you know, and my bucket, and I kiss her once again. That's routine. You understand. Then I get in the car." Now, he lives near all the railroad tracks, and if he misses the crossing, there's a hundred cars go by, it's a fifteen minute wait. You're docked one hour if you come one minute late.

So now he's describing the scene that is absolutely suspenseful. It's exciting. Is he going to make it on time? And so he hits a certain spot beating that train, knows just when to do it. He makes it just on time. And it's so dramatic as he describes that morning.

Now I go see a college professor. I'm not putting down intellectuals, I'm just describing to you how abstract some academicians can be. I said, "Tell me what your day's like." "Well, I'm in class, and I'm teaching Aristotle 101." Now, all that before is omitted. In short, nothing happened. Whereas, in the case of the utility man, there was so much drama and life.

The Dickensian details are what I look for. Dickens, of course. What made Dickens so great, aside from the social conscience, is the details, the telling details, you see?

Sometimes work, you know, is a chore. For many people that's so. Now the assembly line worker, thanks to the UAW, is thirty and out. Thirty years and then you get a pension. And he dreams, oh, he longs for the time he can be thirty and out, and he can go fishing, he can take it easy, to go. What does he do all day at work? He shoots that welding gun and all day, twenty pounds or so, all day in one spot, into a revolving snake, the assembly line. He doesn't see the end product. And we know that in Sweden they have teams that do the car from beginning to end.

He's longing for that day. He wants to retire. Now, that's not the same, say, with the professor, or someone else who loves his work, who reaches the age of seventy, seventy-five. There's no need for him to retire. He's still got it—I'm saying this for personal reasons, obviously. But the point is he is forced to retire at sixty-five or even seventy. So it depends upon the nature of the work. One loved his work; the other loathed it. They had to make a living, you see. But the point is, what do you do during the day for some lines of work? What do you fantasize for yourself?

I describe a guy named Conrad [Conrad Swibel, p. 274], a meter reader. Now, he has it made. "Tell me what was your day's like?" "Well,

I got this flashlight and I go into the basement of homes to check the meter," you know?

"And, well, I'll tell you, sir, there are two things that I'm involved with. Dogs and women." The first is reality, the second is fantasy. So I said, "Let's start with the dogs." He said, "Well, dogs, those damned dogs." In fact, he was cursing. "They come at you. Poodles are the worst," he says. "They gnaw at you. And one is gnawing at my foot, and I want to hit him with my flashlight, and the woman says, 'What are you doin' to my dog?' 'Lady, what's he doing to my *leg*?' " So that's the first thing. And sometimes he's following the lady of the house down the stairs. And the little dog is right behind her. "So now and then I just kick that little dog to make up for the one I missed over there."

I said, "Well, now let's talk about women." He says, "Well, that's just it—it hasn't happened, you understand, but I think it might, you see, especially in the suburbs. You got that hope.

"I'm walking in the summer in a back yard, there's the lady of the house lying, and she's oooo, kinda good-looking. Young housewife lying there. Getting the sun. Lying on a blanket. She's in a bikini. She's lying on her stomach in a bikini to get the sun on her back, and she opens her bra. You know how her bra's open to get the sun on her back without the strap on?

"So I creep up very, very slowly. When I'm close to her, I holler, 'Gas man!' She turns around and bawls me out. 'Why didn't you announce yourself?' See, I get bawled out an awful lot, but it makes the day go faster."

Now making the day go faster is what it's about. It depends upon the job. How a person feels about the job. Does it do something to his spirit? In many cases, you know, it diminishes it. One girl in the book said, "Jobs are not big enough for people." So we're talking about the nature of work itself, aren't we?

Finding the Interviewees, Editing the Interviews

My batting average is pretty good. I save more than half I've interviewed. Yeah, which is a very good batting average. It's not just seeing somebody. It's seeing somebody special.

That is—an ordinary person, so-called. I'm not the celebrity. All areas of work. You have executives in there too. But mostly seeing somebody who is able to say something that his peer or neighbor can't. Sometimes they'd say something to me and experience the shock of recognition. "Why don't you see Florence at the end of the block?"

Why? Florence is like *she* is. Part of the same stratum, economically, socially, academically. Not different. But Florence happened to be somebody who was able to articulate what all the others feel but couldn't express. She speaks for them, and so it's the Florences I see.

And the Florence also is a storyteller, a raconteur. Many people happen to be natural storytellers. They haven't been asked these questions before in their lives. Generally, the questions asked are about celebrities, right? Asked about this or that or about a headline. And so when you ask them that and you start a conversation— it's not an interview, not a Q & A. On the contrary. My questions often are wiped out in the book itself. They're kept in only when it serves a certain purpose: humor, a laugh, or an insight. But aside from that, it's a conversation, having a cup of coffee with that person.

I might meet that person by accident. Sometimes—I was on the station WFMT for many years, where you heard me. And your brother. Now and then the subject of race came up, and I had people on, and I had certain opinions, of course. I got a call from a woman who was furious. She says, "You think you know. You don't know what it's like to live here. You know who you sound like? My mother." And I said, "What's your mother's phone number?" And the mother happened to be a woman, Elizabeth Chapin. That's her name. She's in my first book, *Division Street: America.* And she's an old Chicagoan. And she was wonderful. I got a good meal out of it too. But the fact is that through this woman who bawled me out, I found this person I have in the book, not in *Working* but it's all related to *Working* as well.

In *The Good War*, for example, the World War II book, I'm interviewing a fantastic guy. His name was Bob Rasmus. He's one of the best in the book. This young kid, mother's boy, was very tall, and he got to be a point man. The point man's the guy who comes out first in the infantry. The most visible, most vulnerable.

He's scared stiff, and he's relating this and it's a wonderful story. As he's leaving he says, "It's a funny thing about the war. I met a guy the other day standing on the platform, on State Street, waiting for the lights to change. He looked at me, he said, 'Are you Bob Rasmus?' I said, 'Red Pendergast.' We were together in the platoon, forty years before." Red Pendergast is a good story. Like Kurt Vonnegut. He was in Dresden—a P.O.W. as the Allies bombed the city.

I said, "Can I see Red?" So he gave me his number. I saw Red Pendergast, and that became a sequence called "Brief Encounter."

So that's how I work. Hunches. And so in *Working* too. Somebody told me about somebody else and I went on from there.

As far as how much I edit out, it all depends. Some are longer than others. I and my publisher, André, edit it together. And it's remarkable how we come out almost the same. You know, on the same wavelength. But the editing is generally mine. Editing is half the job.

A lot of this conversation is digressing and wandering and coming back to the point. Sometimes digression is good, but you also get a lot that is repeated. So what you do is you edit. Now, I do not change any word. The words are the words of the person talking to me. I don't add my words. I have a little introduction to each one and that's it.

My point of view is in the introduction. This book is about work, the violent nature of the work. You're kicking the dog around and you get ulcers and . . . that's my own part.

I never invent words. The words are theirs. Sometimes you juxtapose the sequence in which they said it because, is there a rule? There's no rule. It's not written in stone that you start this with, "Where you were born?" You start almost anywhere. It depends upon the whole situation. "What is it about the Depression," I'd say to them, "that most affects you?" He says, "I hate rotten bananas, because when I was a kid, we had rotten bananas." Or, "I can't stand smashed sardines."

The editing highlights it, just as with a playwright. The playwright highlights the truth. And so when you put down what that person said, you synthesize it. I may change the sequence because it could begin anywhere. No one has to start with birth. Or when you get up in the morning. I did that with this utilities guy, but it may not work with someone else. It could be anywhere, you could start almost anywhere.

Editing is the key to the whole thing. First, it's finding the person; then the conversation. How do you find people? Again, accident. Word of mouth is the big thing.

People I know about. I knew about Rick. I knew about Bill, and you, because you were WFMT listeners. I also knew who your father was. And so of course the chapter: father and son. Then I went out and found two other fathers and sons and then that's a sequence [pp. 545–589] (Robert Baird and his two sons in *Hard Times* are actually Tom, Bill, and Rick Ayers. Studs revisited the father–son theme in *Working*, pp. 545–589.)

The Organization of *Working*

So, it seems almost biblical. It began with the preface. It was a mason; we think of the Tower of Babel, the mason; the carpenter, Jesus; from the year one, the farmer. So it begins with these three. The mason, the carpenter, the farmer.

That leads to the question of who really makes the wheels go around? It's the noncelebrated people. My favorite quote from Bertolt Brecht, a German playwright and poet—kids know of him because of *The Threepenny Opera*; they know him because the song "Mack the Knife" is from *The Threepenny Opera*—is this poem which asked: Who built the seven gates of Thebes? You know? Who carried those crags of rock that built the thing? If I would ask somebody, "Who built the pyramids?" the first reaction would be "Pharaoh!"

But Pharaoh didn't lift a finger. Mrs. Pharaoh's nails were as immaculately manicured as Elizabeth Taylor's. No, who built it? Anonymous slaves down through the centuries built it. Who are these people?

He asks further, "When the Chinese wall was built, where did the masons go to lunch? When Caesar conquered Gaul"—we got this in Latin I, Caesar's *Commentary*—"was there not even a cook in the army? Who would it be? Who were the others?"

And the big one—I remember this as a kid in elementary school—

the date 1588: Sir Francis Drake conquered the Spanish Armada. He did? By himself? You mean he waved a sword and the Spaniards gave up?

And so Brecht asks in the poem, "When the Armada sank, we read that King Philip wept." King Philip of Spain wept. And he asked the big question, "Were there no other tears?" Who were these others that shed these other tears?

Advice for Students Using the Book

As for students using *Working* today, they must think about what it is like for those who had done the jobs, old ones or new, through their lives. All of my oral histories are connected, because they deal with memory.

Hard Times, in which your brothers and father appeared, is memory of what it was like, especially in the case of your father, who was an executive. He started out as a worker. And what it would mean to be the sons of him in a certain moment in the sixties and seventies. And so what is it like to do that sort of job?

With *Working*, as with the other books, it's putting yourself in the shoes of the other. One of the sadnesses of our day—this applies to a high school student, to all students—through no fault of their own, they may not know too much about what it was like. History itself, you know, is under the gun, because, thanks to technology and to sound bites and TV, *now* is what counts. There is no yesterday. What happened yesterday is forgotten. That's what these guys are banking on, the Neanderthals of the Republican party. I was listening last night—one of the guys on TV. In his outrageous comments, he assumed the average public has the intelligence of a twelve-year-old. And I don't mean to insult twelve-year-olds. There is no past. You see?

Someone will ask, "Is that actually true?" It's true to that person. It happened to him. That's why he/she remembers it. There's a line in the great novel *The Grapes of Wrath* by John Steinbeck about the Great Depression. It's about the Okie families, the dust bowl, and they are moved off their farms, and they've got to go to California, hoping they'll find something there. They run into a guy coming back from California at some jungle camp. He says, "You guys are going there? I'm going back home. I want my kid to starve at home. There's no work there." Tom Joad, the hero—Henry Fonda played it in the movie—he says to the preacher, "Is that guy telling the truth?" He replies, "The truth for him." For us? Well, we'll find out.

And so they're telling the truth for themselves. And that to me is pretty good stuff. When you have enough of them saying that, it's basically true. A fact here or there may be off, that's not the point.

A big reward for me is when somebody stops me on the street and says, "I'll never again talk that way to a waitress. . . . I'll never again talk that way to one of those truck drivers on the interstate," because I describe what their work is like.

Remember the movie *Five Easy Pieces*? Now, I hope the students of Rick have seen *Five Easy Pieces*, or maybe they're too young for that, because that's also another time. It's of the seventies, isn't it? It was a great movie, but it had a horrible sequence in it. I'm attacking it now because of that scene with the waitress.

For those who haven't seen the movie, it's with Jack Nicholson—the acting is very good. I'm not talking about the acting. I'm talking about this one scene. Jack Nicholson is on his way to Alaska with some friends, and he's disenchanted with things, and he's impatient. And they're going to this little greasy spoon.

We immediately see the waitress. We don't like her. The actress played her as a virago. And he says, "Can I have—can I have a little substitution? Is it possible to have something not on the menu?" She says coldly, "No! What's on the menu, that's there." And he's so furious, he just takes the food and he throws it on the floor. And guess what? The kids in the movie house—I was the oldest there by forty years—kids in the movie house are cheering. And I'm saying, "You little bastards. Have you ever thought about this woman who is the waitress? What's her day like?"

Why is she a waitress? Does she have varicose veins? Because very often, you know, waitresses and flight attendants are inclined to that because of the walk back and forth. Yeah, being on your feet. That's in a sequence (in *Working*) called "Footwork." The mailman is part of that too.

But so, as she's doing this work, does she have a headache? How many Seconals or how many Tylenols did she take that day? Or why is she a waitress? 'Cause she needed cash, tips and all. Is her husband not working, or dead? Is her girl in trouble? Is the boy on dope? Did she have a fight with the cook? We don't know a thing about her, except she's this virago. That's the part that made me furious about this movie.

Changing the World

Lots of people talk about the world, "Nothing I can do about it. Who am I? You can't beat city hall." The fact is that many of the people in these books I have are people who do try to beat city hall. These are people who—like I mentioned Florence. There's an actual Florence. Florence Scala.

She's in the very first book, *Division Street: America*. She tried to save a community in Chicago. It was a multicultural community, primarily Italian, but there were Latino people and a few black people there. It was a cultural group that was wonderful. However, the cement lobby and the mayor then thought, well, this is a good place for expressways and highways and for UIC (University of Illinois at Chicago).

So today the university is like a fortress. I have nothing against the college. It's got wonderful teachers, and the students are fine. But I'm talking about the structure itself, of the place. It destroyed the community. Her story appears in many forms in all the books.

I seek out the ones who say no! "No, we're gonna make a change. I do have a say." As in the case of one woman—Mary Lou Wolf is her name. She is the mother of nine kids. She is a Roman Catholic. She says, "There's nothing I can do." One day she meets this young priest. The young priest is an activist. A group of powerful politicians and industrialists are forcing an expressway through the community in which she lives, an expressway that would, in effect, destroy the community. And people are just crying and crying, and whose home is gonna go first? Whose block? So she asks what I call the impertinent question: "Whose home has to go to begin with? Why do we need this thing? We don't need this expressway." She formed a group, and the group stopped the expressway. And from then on she became interested in other things— the war and other matters—that changed her life. So sometimes you must act locally. Act locally, think globally. This was a case in point.

The key word is community. Sense of community. In all the works. Not just *Working*, all the books. There's a sense of community.

You know, the sixties have been criticized a great deal. The sixties, I loved the sixties. Sure, there were excesses. Of course. But the young people in the sixties had causes outside themselves, whether it was civil rights or it was the Vietnam War. They had a true community sense.

Now somebody says, "I count." And so the sixties had the phrase used by young activists—"participatory democracy." The key word is *participatory*. When this country was formed, it was on the basis of participatory democracy. The great writer, the pamphleteer, was Tom Paine. And Tom Paine always spoke of that person taking part. Sam Adams. He was an agitator up in Boston, and he destroyed somebody's property, somebody's tea, through the Tea Party. Well, the idea was participatory democracy.

And one of the things we have—we have many grassroots groups in the country, and they're wonderful, but we need more. Participation does something to the person. This applies to the students. When you become part of something, a cause in which you believe, something involves you. It could be environment. It could be anything that's through the community in which you live. It could be a developer taking over. It could be the guys dumping harmful stuff in the community. When you take part, you suddenly realize you count. You count! Because for many— there's a lack of self-esteem.

And so we're told, "You've got to make it on your own." The key word is competition. What does that mean, competition? It means when you get right down to it: beating the other guy. Dog eat dog. The word we rarely hear these days is cooperation—community.

The Legacy of the Thirties

The thirties was a tremendous period. Of course it was a hard time, but also it was a government at the time that believed in remedies. You see— I'm not saying that Franklin D. Roosevelt was a saint. But he had a sense of history, he surrounded himself with people, men and women, who knew something was needed over and beyond.

Now, we're talking about the free market today, private enterprise, which fell on its face, and the stock market. Everyone is talking about how great the free market is. Well, back in 1929, something happened. The big boys slipped on a banana peel. And there was a crash. There was a stock market crash. They didn't know what hit them. The Depression began officially in 1929, October, with that stock market crash. There was a depression before that, a big agricultural depression. Suddenly millions became unemployed. So I went to see the wise man of Wall Street, the same kind telling us things are great now. He was an adviser to Harry Truman, to Kennedy, to LBJ. I said, "What happened that day?" "I don't know."

This old guy, recalling 1929, says, "I don't know. The thing just happened. The ticker tape was going all night, and John D. Rockefeller was buying thousands of shares of common stock. Down it went. J. P. Morgan was buying thousands of shares of common stock. Down it went. Men were jumping out of windows. We didn't know—we waited for some kind of an announcement." And I thought to myself, this wise man is waiting for some kind of announcement. From whom? From God? He went on, "Well, the announcement came from big government. They saved our hides."

Ironically, the very ones whose daddies' and granddaddies' asses were saved by big government are the ones who most condemn big government. Ronald Reagan is a good case. Now, some of the kids' parents, I'm sure, voted for Reagan. I must tell you a story about Ronnie Reagan, who condemned big government. He came from a town called Dixon, Illinois. And that town was fully unemployed during the Depression. His father got a job, a government job, on the WPA (Work Projects Administration). WPA was part of the New Deal of Roosevelt. It was giving people work. The town was saved by the WPA. That's forgotten.

It's like someone who's able to climb up a ladder—like you have a black guy who is against affirmative action, like Clarence Thomas or this guy Connerly in California. People know about Ward Connerly. It's a guy who climbs up the ladder thanks to affirmative action and kicks the ladder out from under him. Well, that's the worst loathsome kind of creature you could think of.

I'm not now canonizing the government, but the fact is there's a need sometimes. As with affirmative action—there's a need to rectify what is rotten and wrong, to straighten out the crooked places, to use a scriptural phrase of some sort. That's in *Hard Times*, how the WPA saved the lives of so many people. You see, we're told about welfare bums, aren't we? Welfare bums. In those days the word was Relief. Overwhelmingly white. Today, for that matter, most welfare recipients are white, most single mothers are white. But in the old days it was called Relief. They didn't use phrases like "underclass." They never used that phrase.

The fact is then, too, you had [the Relief] people coming in the house to see if there was a man in the house. There were single mothers then. The guy is not working. A while back I said, "What's a kid like whose father comes home with a tool chest on his shoulder?" Well, that carpenter comes home, doesn't work for five years in that Great Depression. So what does he do? He's frustrated. He gets drunk. There are fights with his wife, with the son, father and son—he leaves home out of shame or something like that. So you have a single parent all of a sudden. You had that then too. But there was a government that was at least interested in them and didn't condemn them as being a subculture or something.

The Changing Face of Work

So that's part of it. That's what I mean by forgetting our own history, remembering our history. And it applies to working as well. Now, working is changing today, with more and more technology and the computer, God help us. Although the computer's doing good things, we know. There is always the danger that we may become more like the machine. For years we had machines imitating humans. In fact, in *Working*, one guy, a young auto worker [Gary Bryner, p. 187] is describing an auto plant in Ohio where General Motors is trying to compete with the foreign small cars and made this car. What was it called? The Vega. Terrible car. It flopped.

There's a union leader saying, "We have an assembly line, but there's something new. There's a robot at the beginning of the line. And that robot does what we do. It bends over. It comes back. But the robot doesn't strike. The robot doesn't protest. It doesn't take time out to eat. And we've become like this, but the robot imitates us."

But now since it's more and more computerized, we may be imitating the robot. I'll give you an example. Now here are funny stories.

The Atlanta airport is a very modern airport, and at the gate there are trains that take you to the concourse of your choice. Other airports are like that. You get on that train. And I was on that train.

You hear a voice. You don't see the person. You hear a voice. You come on the train. There're a few seats. You stand. It moves very smoothly. Silence. Dead silence. And this voice says, imitating a robotic voice, "Concourse one," monotone. "For Fort Worth, Dallas, Lubbock. Concourse two, Springfield, Peoria." One voice. There's silence.

And just as the doors are about to close, pneumatic doors, a young couple, maybe honeymooners, come in and squeeze through the doors and just make it. And the voice, without missing a beat, intones, "Because of late entry we're delayed 30 seconds." Guess what happens. What happens? At that moment people look at that couple, as though they were terrorists. Look at this couple. They are shrinking like that.

Now, I happened to have had a couple of drinks, to steel myself for occasions of this sort. So I holler out, cupping my hands like an old-time train caller, "George Orwell, your time has come and gone!" You laugh, but nobody laughed then. They looked at me, and suddenly I joined the young couple at the foot of Calvary. And there we are. So just then, I see a woman sitting there. She's a Latino woman, she's talking Spanish to her friend. And there's a little baby in her lap, about a year-old baby. So I looked at the baby. After all, you know, I've had a few drinks. I looked at the baby. Cupping my hands because my breath may have been a hundred proof, I say to the baby, "What is your opinion of all this? What do you think?" And the baby giggles, especially when she sees an old nut. I say, "Thank God, a human voice." So there's hope.

There seems to be less personal connection today. For example, I make a telephone call. I want to call Charlie, a friend of mine, Charlie Andrews. In the old days a human voice picked up the phone, "Charlie's not in." Or if nobody answers, I call again. This time a voice answers, and the voice says, "If you want such and such, push one. If you want so and so, push two. Push three, push four." By this time I don't know who the hell it was I called in the first place. What happened to the human voice, huh? I talk about that in *Working*. And the irony is that I'm such a hypocrite. I use a tape recorder. I'm on the radio!

I'm really an ingrate. But often I make a mistake. I press the wrong button. I've done this so often. I've lost hundreds of tapes. I've lost Bertrand Russell. I've lost Martha Graham, the great dancer. I lost Vanessa Redgrave, the British actress. No, I saved Bertrand Russell. I almost lost him. I lost the others though. So that's part of it.

Here's the other part. I'm not condemning technology. Let's get this straight. I'm not against the refrigerator, because where else can I cool—freeze—my martini glass? Right? And I'm not against the washing machine, because I'd have to see women slapping clothes against wet rocks.

I had a quintuple bypass operation. Yeah. Quintuple. About three years ago. And I was saved by the skilled hands of a surgeon, but also by technology. So you see how ungrateful I am?

I'm not a Luddite. Luddites were those people who took part in the agricultural revolt in England in the eighteenth century, when the farm machinery was coming and putting the farm laborers out of work. Now, that's the same thing that's happening now. But there's a need to retrain these people. You don't put them out of work like that. You don't fire them like that. And we have that happening more and more, what with multinationals taking over companies, moving elsewhere.

But now they say the new jobs are information jobs. Maybe work itself should be redefined. Work is always judged by how much you make, or by productivity. Maybe work is something else too. Maybe a housewife should be paid. Now, this is revolutionary. A housewife's work is what? Raising a human being. What's more important than that? You know what a housewife does. A million different things. Maybe she'd be respected more if she were paid. Maybe students going to school should be paid. In some societies that's what they do.

Maybe they can pay you, assuming that the education is open and multicultural, in every way. If we create a real humanistic education, once you have this education, you're much richer as a person, and your richness becomes part of the community. So maybe—yes, maybe in a healthy educational system, and there's no reason it shouldn't be—students could be paid. Absolutely. In other words, work must be redefined. Work can be expanded over and beyond the making of things. And now, we have things making things.

Talking is so important. Talking about things that concern us—we don't talk about our lives really. Everything is diverted from our felt lives. What is the news today? Trivia is news to a great extent. We watch *Entertainment Tonight* at six o'clock.

I'm not against Michael Jordan. I admire Michael Jordan, of course. But he's not the beginning and end of the world, of the human race. The American male on a bus Monday morning after a Sunday football game talks about that game with such knowledge and detail. But ask him about Africa? He wouldn't know what the hell it's about. He thinks Africa's one country.

If we had as much knowledge of the world, and interest in it, as we do of sports, I mean commercial sports, we'd be the most enlightened country ever. But we're not. Far from that.

And so this is what we're talking about. Many people said they've changed their lives because of the book. They decided to think about what they were doing again. So I must say that has bolstered my ego very much.

Editing Lesson

How does the interviewer edit the piece to get a "Studs Terkel" style narrative? I had the experience of being in the presence of Studs when he did some of his editing. While carrying on a side conversation with me, being distracted by the phone and other events, Studs sat and edited the draft I had made of the interview John had conducted with him. He started by having me read parts and giving me suggestions for clarification, smoothing out parts, rephrasing others. Of course, this was an interview with him so he had wider rights to make such changes.

Soon, however, he tired of my slow note-taking and took out a pen while moving the transcript to his lap. With great speed and concentration, he read the transcript, mumbled lines over to himself, and then with deft hand crossed out, tightened, and clarified points. He did this without tiring for 20 pages.

Have students look at the versions that follow of just one page and study the ways that the text has changed through subsequent editing. The first one is the raw tape transcript. The second is my version, cleaned up from the tape transcript. I tried to take out the questions and make a running narrative. The third is the page with Terkel's marking on it. The last is the final version that appears in the interview above. Notice that a subhead is placed in the middle of the page to signal a new theme or direction.

1) Raw Transcription of Interview Tape

. . . writer, the pamphleteer, was Tom Paine. And Tom Paine always spoke of that person taking part. Sam Adams. He was an agitator up in Boston, and he destroyed somebody's property, somebody's tea, through the Tea Party, you see? Well, the idea was participatory democracy.

John Ayers: And [inaudible]

Studs Terkel: And one of the things we have—we have many grassroots groups in the country, and they're wonderful, but we need more.

JA: Right.

ST: [inaudible]

JA: And didn't de Tocqueville also . . .

ST: What's that?

JA: Didn't de Tocqueville really stress that too? That America was about active participation by everyday citizens.

ST: Participation does something to the person. This applies to the students. You may think it's just agitate. No, it isn't. When you become part of something, a cause in which you believe, something involves you. It could be environment. It could be anything. That's through the community in which you live. It could be a developer taking over. It could be the guys dumping harmful stuff in the community around there. When you take part, you suddenly realize you count. You count! Because there's many—there's a lack of self-esteem. And so we're told, "You've got to make it on your own." See, we're [inaudible].

JA: Individualism.

ST: The key word is competition. What does that mean, competition? [Inaudible] called the free market. [Inaudible] feeding somebody else. Feeding somebody else talks about winning together, a community improving itself. Now I sound like a preacher. But in a sense we can't help it. That's what it really is, you see?

ST: [Inaudible] You see—I'm not saying that Franklin D. Roosevelt was a saint, but no. But he had a sense of his—, to surrounded himself with people, men and women, who knew something was needed over and beyond. Now [inaudible], we're talking about the free market today, and the stock market. By God, and he's getting told that. Well, then it was the same way, and then something happened. People slipped on a banana peel, the big boys did. And there was a crash. There was a stock market crash. They didn't know what hit them. There was an official—the Depression began officially in 1929, October, with that stock market crash. There was a depression before that, a big agricultural depression. But that—then people were unemployed, millions unemployed. So I went to see the wise men of Wall Street, the same kind telling us things are great now. I went to see this wise man of Wall Street who was an advisor . . .

2) My First Edited Version

. . . writer, the pamphleteer, was Tom Paine. And Tom Paine always spoke of that person taking part. Sam Adams. He was an agitator up in Boston, and he destroyed somebody's property, somebody's tea, through the Tea Party, you see? Well, the idea was participatory democracy.

And one of the things we have—we have many grassroots groups in the country, and they're wonderful, but we need more. Participation does something to the person. This applies to the students. You may think it's just agitate. No, it isn't. When you become part of something, a cause in which you believe, something involves you. It could be environment. It could be anything. That's through the community in which you live. It could be a developer taking over. It could be the guys dumping harmful stuff in the community around there. When you take part, you suddenly realize you count. You count! Because for many—there's a lack of self-esteem. And so we're told, "You've got to make it on your own." The key word is competition. What does that mean, competition? But now we've got something called the free market. But feeding somebody else. Feeding somebody else talks about winning together, a community improving itself. Now I sound like a preacher. But in a sense we can't help it. That's what it really is, you see?

The Thirties was a tremendous period. Of course it was a hard time, but also it was a government at the time that believed in remedies. You see—I'm not saying that Franklin D. Roosevelt was a saint, but no. But he had a sense of his—, to surrounded himself with people, men and women, who knew something was needed over and beyond. Now, we're talking about the free market today, and the stock market. By God, and he's getting told that. Well, then it was the same way, and then something happened. People slipped on a banana peel, the big boys did. And there was a crash. There was a stock market crash. They didn't know what hit them. There was an official—the Depression began officially in 1929, October, with that stock market crash. There was a depression before that, a big agricultural depression. But that—then people were unemployed, millions unemployed. So I went to see the wise men of Wall Street, the same kind telling us things are great now. I went to see this wise man of Wall Street who was an advisor . . .

3) Hand Edits by Studs Terkel

writer, the pamphleteer, was Tom Paine. And Tom Paine always spoke of that person taking part. Sam Adams. He was an agitator up in Boston, and he destroyed somebody's property, somebody's tea, through the Tea Party, you see? Well, the idea was participatory democracy.

And one of the things we have - we have many grassroots groups in the country, and they're wonderful, but we need more. Participation does something to the person. This applies to the students. You may think it's just agitate. No, it isn't. When you become part of something, a cause in which you believe, something involves you. It could be environment. It could be anything. That's through the community in which you live. It could be a developer taking over. It could be the guys dumping harmful stuff in the community around there. When you take part, you suddenly realize you count. You count! Because for many - there's a lack of self-esteem. And so we're told, "You've got to make it on your own." The key word is competition. What does that mean, competition? But now we've got something called the free market. But feeding somebody else. Feeding somebody else talks about winning together, a community improving itself. Now I sound like a preacher. But in a sense we can't help it. That's what it really is, you see?

The Thirties was a tremendous period. Of course it was a hard time, but also it was a government at the time that believed in remedies. You see - I'm not saying that Franklin D. Roosevelt was a saint, but no. But he had a sense of his, to surrounded himself with people, men and women, who knew something was needed over and beyond private enterprise. Now, we're talking about the free market today, and the stock market. By God, we're getting told that. Well, then it was the same way, and then something happened. People slipped on a banana peel, the big boys did. And there was a crash. There was a stock market crash. They didn't know what hit them. There was an official. The Depression began officially in 1929, October, with that stock market crash. There was a depression before that, a big agricultural depression. But that—then people were unemployed, millions unemployed. So I went to see the wise men of Wall Street, the same kind telling us things are great now. I went to see this wise man of Wall Street who was an advisor

4) Final Edited Version

. . . writer, the pamphleteer, was Tom Paine. And Tom Paine always spoke of that person taking part. Sam Adams. He was an agitator up in Boston, and he destroyed somebody's property, somebody's tea, through the Tea Party. Well, the idea was participatory democracy.

And one of the things we have—we have many grassroots groups in the country, and they're wonderful, but we need more. Participation does something to the person. This applies to the students. When you become part of something, a cause in which you believe, something involves you. It could be environment. It could be anything that's through the community in which you live. It could be a developer taking over. It could be the guys dumping harmful stuff in the community. When you take part, you suddenly realize you count. You count! Because for many—there's a lack of self-esteem.

And so we're told, "You've got to make it on your own." The key word is competition. What does that mean, competition? It means when you get right down to it: beating the other guy. Dog eat dog. The word we rarely hear these days is cooperation—community. . . .

The Legacy of the Thirties

The thirties was a tremendous period. Of course it was a hard time, but also it was a government at the time that believed in remedies. You see— I'm not saying that Franklin D. Roosevelt was a saint. But he had a sense of history, he surrounded himself with people, men and women, who knew something was needed over and beyond.

Now, we're talking about the free market today, private enterprise, which fell on its face, and the stock market. Everyone is talking about how great the free market is. Well, back in 1929, something happened. The big boys slipped on a banana peel. And there was a crash. There was a stock market crash. They didn't know what hit them. The Depression began officially in 1929, October, with that stock market crash. There was a depression before that, a big agricultural depression. Suddenly millions became unemployed. So I went to see the wise man of Wall Street, the same kind telling us things are great now. He was an adviser . . .

IV

RESOURCES

Oral History Association

For ongoing updates on practices in oral history, as well as for resources that support student research and standards in gathering oral history, contact the Oral History Association:

OHA
Dickinson College
P.O. Box 1773
Carlisle, PA 17013
Telephone: 717-245-1036
Fax: 717-245-1046
E-mail: OHA@dickinson.edu
    Following are some useful materials adapted from the OHA:

ORAL HISTORY STANDARDS (ADOPTED 1989)

Since its founding in 1967 the Oral History Association (OHA) has grappled constantly with developing and promoting professional standards for oral historians. This has been no easy task, given the creative, dynamic nature of the field. The OHA has sought to encourage the creation of recorded interviews that are as complete, verifiable, and usable as possible, and to discourage both inadequate interviewing and the misuse of oral history. Yet it recognizes that oral historians cannot afford to suppress ingenuity and inspiration nor to ignore new developments in scholarship and technology.

The OHA issued its first "goals and guidelines" in 1968, broadly stating the principles, rights, and obligations that all interviewees, interviewers, and sponsoring institutions needed to take into consideration. Then, in 1979, at the prompting of various granting agencies, leaders of the OHA met at the Wingspread Conference Center in Racine, Wisconsin, to produce a set of "evaluation guidelines." These guidelines have since provided invaluable assistance to oral history projects of all sizes and purposes. Organized in checklist form, they offered reminders of the myriad issues involved in conducting, processing, and preserving oral history interviews. Not every guideline applied to every project, but taken together they provided a common ground for dialogue among oral historians.

Over the next decade, new issues arose that the earlier guidelines had not addressed. When the need for revision became apparent, the OHA decided against convening another special meeting, as was done at Wingspread, and instead appointed four committees to examine those sections of the evaluation guidelines that required revision or entirely new material. After a year's work, the committees presented their proposals to members of the association at a series of sessions at the annual meeting in Galveston, Texas, in October 1989. The revised committee reports were then discussed, amended, and adopted by a vote of the membership at the general business meeting. During the next year, the chairs of the four evaluation guidelines committees analyzed, revised, and expanded the Goals and Guidelines into a new Statement of Principles and Standards to accompany the Evaluation Guidelines. Finally, they offered these standards for amendment and adoption by the OHA membership at the annual meeting in Cambridge, Massachusetts, in November 1990.

If this process sounds convoluted, it was. But its many stages were designed deliberately to foster thoughtful debate among the widest cross-section of oral history practitioners. As a result, the new standards and guidelines more specifically addressed the needs of independent and unaffiliated researchers, as well as those of the larger oral history programs and archives. They dealt with the problems and potentials of videotaped interviews. They raised issues about the use of oral history projects in the classroom by teachers and students. By the end of the process, the OHA felt assured that it had listened to all sides and had reached a workable consensus.

The most intense discussions predictably dealt with ethical issues. A greater awareness of the effects of race, class, gender, ethnicity, and culture on interviewing, together with a heightened concern over the impact that the oral history projects might have on the communities in which the interviews were conducted, were woven into both the Evaluation Guidelines and the Statement of Principles and Standards. The new guidelines and standards encouraged oral historians to make their interviews accessible to the community and to consider sharing the rewards and recognition that might result from their projects with their interviewees. They also sanctioned the use of anonymous interviews, although only in "extremely sensitive" circumstances.

All of those who labored in the preparation of the Statement of Principles and Standards and the Evaluation Guidelines trust that they will offer positive assistance to anyone conducting oral history interviews. While these guidelines and standards provide a basis for peer judgment and review, their success will ultimately depend more on the willingness of individual oral historians and oral history projects to apply them to their own work.

PRINCIPLES AND STANDARDS OF THE ORAL HISTORY ASSOCIATION

The Oral History Association promotes oral history as a method of gathering and preserving historical information through recorded interviews with participants in past events and ways of life. It encourages those who produce and use oral history to recognize certain principles, rights, technical standards, and obligations for the creation and preservation of source material that is authentic, useful, and reliable. These include obligations to the interviewee, to the profession, and to the public, as well as mutual obligations between sponsoring organizations and interviewers.

Oral history interviews are conducted by people with a range of affiliations and sponsorship for a variety of purposes: to create archival records, for individual research, for community and institutional projects, and for publications and media productions. While these principles and standards provide a general framework for guiding professional conduct, their application may vary according to the nature of specific oral history projects. Regardless of the purpose of the interviews, oral history should be conducted in the spirit of critical inquiry and social responsibility, and with a recognition of the interactive and subjective nature of the enterprise.

Responsibility to Interviewees

1. Interviewees should be informed of the purposes and procedures of oral history in general and of the aims and anticipated uses of the particular projects to which they are making their contribution.

2. Interviewees should be informed of the mutual rights in the oral history process, such as editing, access restrictions, copyrights, prior use, royalties, and the expected disposition and dissemination of all forms of the record, including the potential for electronic distribution.

3. Interviewees should be informed that they will be asked to sign a legal release. Interviews should remain confidential until interviewees have given permission for their use.

4. Interviewers should guard against making promises to interviewees that they may not be able to fulfill, such as guarantees of publication and control over future uses of interviews after they have been made public. In all future uses, however, good faith efforts should be made to honor the spirit of the interviewee's agreement.

5. Interviews should be conducted in accord with any prior agreements made with the interviewee, and such preferences and agreements should be documented for the record.

6. Interviewers should work to achieve a balance between the objectives of the project and the perspectives of the interviewees. They should be sensitive to the diversity of social and cultural experiences, and to the implications of race, gender, class, ethnicity, age, religion, and sexual orientation. They should encourage interviewees to respond in their own style and language, and to address issues that reflect their concerns. Interviewers should fully explore all appropriate areas of inquiry with the interviewee and not be satisfied with superficial responses.

7. Interviewers should guard against possible exploitation of interviewees and be sensitive to the ways in which their interviews might be used. Interviewers must respect the right of the interviewee to refuse to discuss certain subjects, to restrict access to the interview, or under extreme circumstances even to choose anonymity. Interviewers should clearly explain these options to all interviewees.

8. Interviewers should use the best recording equipment within their means in order to accurately reproduce the interviewee's voice and, if appropriate, other sounds as well as visual images.

9. Given the rapid development of new technologies, interviewees should be informed of the wide range of potential uses of their interviews.

10. Good faith efforts should be made to ensure that the uses of recordings and transcripts comply with both the letter and spirit of the interviewee's agreement.

Responsibility to the Public and to the Profession

1. Oral historians have a responsibility to maintain the highest professional standards in the conduct of their work

and to uphold the standards of the various disciplines and professions with which they are affiliated.

2. In recognition of the importance of oral history to an understanding of the past and of the cost and effort involved, interviewers and interviewees should mutually strive to record candid information of lasting value and to make that information accessible.

3. Interviewees should be selected on the basis of the relevance of their experiences to the subject at hand.

4. Interviewers should possess interviewing skills as well as professional competence or experience with the subject at hand.

5. Regardless of the specific interests of the project, interviewers should attempt to extend the inquiry beyond the specific focus of the project to create as complete a record as possible for the benefit of others.

6. Interviewers should strive to prompt informative dialogue through challenging and perceptive inquiry. They should be grounded in the background of the persons being interviewed and, when possible, should carefully research appropriate documents and secondary sources related to subjects about which the interviewees can speak.

7. Interviewers should make every effort to record their interviews, using the best recording equipment within their means to reproduce accurately the interviewee's voice and, if appropriate, image. They should also collect and record other historical documentation in the possession of the interviewee, including still photographs, print materials, and other sound and moving image recordings, as appropriate.

8. Interviewers should provide complete documentation of their preparation and methods, including the circumstances of the interviews.

9. Interviewers, and when possible, interviewees, should review and evaluate their interviews, including any summaries or transcriptions made from them.

10. With the permission of the interviewees, interviewers

should arrange to deposit their interviews in an archival repository that is capable of both preserving the interviews and eventually making them available for general use. Interviewers should provide basic information about the interviews, including project goals, sponsorship, and funding. Preferably, interviewers should work with repositories prior to the project to determine necessary legal arrangements. If interviewers arrange to retain first use of the interviews, it should be only for a reasonable time prior to public use.

11. Interviewers should be sensitive to the communities from which they have collected their oral histories, taking care not to reinforce thoughtless stereotypes or to bring undue notoriety to the communities. They should take every effort to make the interviews accessible to the communities.

12. Oral history interviews should be used and cited with the same care and standards applied to other historical sources. Users have a responsibility to retain the integrity of the interviewee's voice, neither misrepresenting the interviewee's words nor taking them out of context.

13. Sources of funding or sponsorship of oral history projects should be made public in all exhibits, media presentations, or publications that result from the projects.

14. Interviewers and oral history programs should conscientiously consider how they might share with interviewees and their communities the rewards and recognition that might result from their work.

Responsibility for Sponsoring and Maintaining Archival Institutions

1. Institutions sponsoring and maintaining oral history archives have a responsibility to interviewees, interviewers, the profession, and the public to maintain the highest technical, professional, and ethical standards in the creation

and archival preservation of oral history interviews and related materials.

2. Subject to conditions that interviewees set, sponsoring institutions (or individual collectors) have an obligation to prepare and preserve easily usable records; to keep abreast of rapidly developing technologies for preservation and dissemination; to keep accurate records of the creation and processing of each interview; to identify, index, and catalog interviews.

3. Sponsoring institutions and archives should make known the existence of the interviews open for research through a variety of means, including electronic modes of distribution.

4. Within the parameters of their missions and resources, archival institutions should collect interviews generated by independent researchers and assist interviewers with the necessary legal agreements.

5. Sponsoring institutions should train interviewers, providing them basic instruction in the recording of high fidelity interviews, and if appropriate, other sound and moving image recordings; explaining the objectives of the program to them; informing them of all ethical and legal considerations governing an interview; and making clear to interviewers what their obligations are to the program and to the interviewees.

6. Interviewers and interviewees should receive appropriate acknowledgment for their work in all forms of citation or usage.

7. Archives should make good faith efforts to ensure that use of interview recordings and transcripts, especially in new technologies, complies with both the letter and spirit of the interviewee's agreement.

ORAL HISTORY EVALUATION GUIDELINES
Program/Project Guidelines

PURPOSES AND OBJECTIVES

a. Are the purposes clearly set forth? How realistic are they?

b. What factors demonstrate a significant need for the project?

c. What is the research design? How clear and realistic is it?

d. Are the terms, conditions, and objectives of funding clearly made known to judge the potential effect of such funding on the scholarly integrity of the project? Is the allocation of funds adequate to allow the project goals to be accomplished?

e. How do institutional relationships affect the purposes and objectives?

SELECTION OF RECORDING EQUIPMENT

a. Should the interview be recorded on sound or visual recording equipment?

b. Are the best possible recording equipment and media available within one's budget being used?

c. Are interviews recorded on a medium that meets archival preservation standards?

d. How well has the interviewer mastered use of the equipment upon which the interview will be recorded?

SELECTION OF INTERVIEWERS AND INTERVIEWEES

a. In what ways are the interviewers and interviewees appropriate (or inappropriate) to the purposes and objectives?

b. What are the significant omissions and why were they omitted?

RECORDS AND PROVENANCE

a. What are the policies and provisions for maintaining a record of the provenance of interviews? Are they adequate? What can be done to improve them?

b. How are records, policies, and procedures made known to interviewers, interviewees, staff, and users?

c. How does the system of records enhance the usefulness of the interviews and safeguard the rights of those involved?

AVAILABILITY OF MATERIALS

a. How accurate and specific is the publicizing of the interviews?

b. How is information about interviews directed to likely users? Have new media and electronic modes of distribution been considered in order to publicize materials and make them available?

c. How have the interviews been used?

FINDING AIDS

a. What is the overall design for finding aids [subtitles or markings on tape to help the reader find a particular section of the interview that he/she is interested in reviewing]?

b. Are the finding aids adequate and appropriate?

c. How available are the finding aids?

d. Have new technologies been used to develop the most effective finding aids?

MANAGEMENT, QUALIFICATIONS, AND TRAINING

a. How effective is the management of the program/project?

b. What provisions are there for supervision and staff review?

c. What are the qualifications for staff positions?

d. What are the provisions for systematic and effective training?

e. What improvements could be made in the management of the program/project?

Ethical/Legal Guidelines

What procedures are followed to assure that interviewers/programs recognize and honor their responsibility to the interviewees? Specifically, what procedures are used to assure that:

a. the interviewee is made fully aware of the goals and objectives of the oral history program/project?

b. the interviewee is made fully aware of the various stages of the program/project and the nature of his/her participation at each stage?

c. the interviewee is given the opportunity to respond to questions as freely as possible and is not subjected to stereotyped assumptions based on race, ethnicity, gender, class, or any other social/cultural characteristic?

d. the interviewee understands her/his right to refuse to discuss certain subjects, to seal portions of the interview, or, in extremely sensitive circumstances, even to choose to remain anonymous?

e. the interviewee is fully informed about the potential uses to which the material may be put, including deposit of the interviews in a repository, and publication in print, multimedia or electronic media, the Internet or other emerging technologies, as well as in books, articles, newspapers, magazines, radio or film documentaries, and all forms of public programming?

f. the interviewee is provided a full and easily comprehensible explanation of her/his legal rights before being asked to sign a contract or deed of gift transferring rights, title, and interest in the audio and/or visual tape(s) and transcript(s) to an administering authority or individual?

g. care is taken so that the distribution and use of the material complies with the letter and spirit of the interviewee's agreement?

h. all prior agreements made with the interviewee are honored?

i. the interviewee is fully informed about the potential for and disposition of royalties that might accrue from the use of her/his interview, including all forms of public programming?

j. the interview and any other related materials will remain confidential until the interviewee has released their contents?

What procedures are followed to assure that interviewers/programs recognize and honor their responsibilities to the profession? Specifically, what procedures assure that:

a. the interviewer has considered the potential for public programming and research use of the interviews, and has endeavored to prevent any exploitation of or harm to interviewees?

b. the interviewer is well trained to conduct the interview in a professional manner, including the use of appropriate recording equipment and media?

c. the interviewer is well grounded in the background of the subject(s) to be discussed?

d. the interview will be conducted in a spirit of critical inquiry and that efforts will be made to provide as complete a historical record as possible?

e. the interviewees are selected on the basis of the relevance of their experience to the subject at hand and that an appropriate cross-section of interviewees is selected for any particular project?

f. the interview materials, including recordings, transcripts, and relevant photographic, moving image, and sound documents, as well as agreements and documentation of the interview process, will be placed in a repository after a reasonable period of time, subject to the agreements made with the interviewee; and that the depository will administer their use in accordance with those agreements?

g. the methodologies of the program/project, as well as its goals and objectives, are available for the general public to evaluate?

h. the interview materials have been properly cataloged, including appropriate acknowledgment and credit to the interviewer, and that their availability for research use is made known?

What procedures are followed to assure that interviewers and programs are aware of their mutual responsibilities and obligations? Specifically, what procedures are followed to assure that:

a. interviewers are made aware of the program goals and are fully informed of ethical and legal considerations?
b. interviewers are fully informed of all the tasks they are expected to complete in an oral history project?
c. interviewers are made fully aware of their obligations to the oral history program/sponsoring institution, regardless of their own personal interest in a program/project?
d. programs/sponsoring institutions treat their interviewers equitably, including the establishment of provisions for appropriate compensation and acknowledgment for all products resulting from their work, and support for fieldwork practices consistent with professional standards whenever there is a conflict between the parties to the interview?
e. interviewers are fully informed of their legal rights and of their responsibilities to both the interviewee and to the sponsoring institution?

What procedures are followed to assure that interviewers and programs recognize and honor their responsibilities to the community/public? Specifically, what procedures assure that:

a. the oral history materials, and all works created from them, will be available and accessible to the community that participated in the project?
b. sources of extramural funding and sponsorship are clearly cited for each interview or project?

c. the interviewer and project endeavor not to impose their own values on the community being studied?

d. the tapes and transcripts will not be used in an unethical manner?

Tape Preservation Guidelines

Recognizing the historical significance of the recording for historical and cultural analysis, and the potential uses of oral history interviews in nonprint media, what procedures are followed to assure that:

a. appropriate care and storage of the original ("master") recordings begins immediately after their creation?

b. the original ("master") recordings are duplicated and stored under conditions that are in accordance with accepted archival standards [i.e., stored in closed boxes in a cool, dry, dust-free environment]?

c. original recordings are reduplicated or remastered onto the best preservation media before significant deterioration occurs?

d. every effort is made in duplicating tapes to preserve a faithful facsimile of the interviewee's voice?

e. all transcribing, editing, and other uses are done from a dub, not the master?

Tape/Transcript Processing Guidelines

INFORMATION ABOUT THE PARTICIPANTS

a. Are the names of both interviewer and interviewee clearly indicated on the tape/abstract/transcript and in catalog materials?

b. Is there adequate biographical information about both interviewer and interviewee? Where can it be found?

INTERVIEW INFORMATION

a. Are the tapes, transcripts, time indices, abstracts, and other materials presented for use identified as to the project/program of which they are a part?

b. Are the date and place of the interview indicated on the tape, transcript, time index, and abstract, and in appropriate catalog material?

c. Are there interviewer's statements about the preparation for or circumstances of the interviews? Where? Are they generally available to researchers? How are the rights of the interviewees protected against improper use of such commentaries?

d. Are there records of contracts between the program and the interviewee? How detailed are they? Are they available to researchers? If so, with what safeguards for individual rights and privacy?

INTERVIEW TAPE INFORMATION

a. Is the complete master tape preserved? Are there one or more duplicate copies?

b. If the original or any duplicate has been edited, rearranged, cut, or spliced in any way, is there a record of that action, including by whom and when and for what purposes the action was taken?

c. Do the tape label and appropriate catalog materials show the recording speed, level, and length of the interview? If videotaped, do the tape label and appropriate catalog information show the format (e.g., U-Matic, VHS, 8mm, etc.) and scanning system, and clearly indicate the tracks on which the audio and time code have been recorded?

d. In the absence of transcripts, are there suitable finding aids to give users access to information on tapes? What form do they take? Is there a record of who prepares these finding aids?

e. Are researchers permitted to listen to or view the tapes? Are there any restrictions on the use of the tapes?

INTERVIEW TRANSCRIPT INFORMATION

    a. Is the transcript an accurate record of the tape? Is a careful record kept of each step of processing the transcript, including who transcribed, audited, edited, retyped, and proofread the transcripts in final copy?

    b. Are the nature and extent of changes in the transcript from the original tape made known to the user?

    c. What finding aids have been prepared for the transcript? Are they suitable and adequate? How could they be improved?

    d. Are there any restrictions on access to or use of the transcripts? Are they clearly noted?

    e. Are there any photo materials or other supporting documents for the interview? Do they enhance and supplement the text?

    f. If videotaped, does the transcript contain time references and annotation describing the complementary visuals on the videotape?

Interview Content Guidelines

Does the content of each interview and the cumulative content of the whole collection contribute to accomplishing the objectives of the project/program?

    a. In what particulars does each interview or the whole collection succeed or fall short?

    b. Do audio and visual tapes in the collection avoid redundancy and supplement one another in interview content and focus?

In what ways does the program/project contribute to historical understanding?

    a. In what particulars does each interview or the whole collection succeed or fall short of such contribution?

b. To what extent does the material add fresh information, fill gaps in the existing record, and/or provide fresh insights and perspectives?

c. To what extent is the information reliable and valid? Is it eyewitness or hearsay evidence? How well and in what manner does it meet internal and external tests of corroboration, consistency, and explication of contradictions?

d. What is the relationship of the interview information to existing documentation and historiography?

e. How does the texture of the interview impart detail, richness, and flavor to the historical record?

f. What is the basic nature of the information contributed? Does it consist of facts, perceptions, interpretations, judgments, or attitudes, and how does each contribute to understanding?

g. Are the scope, volume, and the representativeness of the population interviewed appropriate and sufficient to the purpose? Is there enough testimony to validate the evidence without passing the point of diminishing returns? How appropriate is the quantity to the purposes of the study?

h. How do the form and structure of the interviews contribute to making the content information understandable?

i. To what extent does the audio and/or video recording capture unique sound and visual information?

j. Do the visual and other sound elements complement and/or supplement the verbal information? Has the interview captured, with the visual and sound environment, processes, objects, or other individuals?

Interview Conduct Guidelines

USE OF OTHER SOURCES

a. Is the oral history technique the best means of acquiring the information? If not, what other sources exist? Has the

interviewer used them, and has he/she sought to preserve
them if necessary?

b. Has the interviewer made an effort to consult other relevant
oral histories?

c. Is the interview technique of value in supplementing existing sources?

d. Do videotaped interviews complement, not duplicate, existing stills or moving visual images?

INTERVIEWER PREPARATION

a. Is the interviewer well informed about the subjects under
discussion?

b. Are the primary and secondary sources used in preparation
for the interview adequate?

c. Has the interviewer mastered the use of appropriate recording equipment and the field-recording techniques that
insure a clean, high-fidelity recording?

INTERVIEWEE SELECTION AND ORIENTATION

a. Does the interviewee seem appropriate to the subjects discussed?

b. Does the interviewee understand and respond to the interview purposes?

c. Has the interviewee prepared for the interview and assisted in the process?

d. If a group interview, have composition and group dynamics
been considered in selecting participants?

INTERVIEWER-INTERVIEWEE RELATIONS

a. Do interviewer and interviewee motivate each other toward
interview objectives?

b. Is there a balance between empathy and analytical judgment in the interview?

c. If videotaped, is the interviewer/interviewee relationship
maintained despite the presence of a technical crew? Did
the technical personnel understand the nature of a video-

taped oral history interview, as opposed to a scripted pro-duction?

TECHNIQUE AND ADAPTIVE SKILLS

a. In what ways does the interview show that the interviewer has used skills appropriate to (1) the interviewee's condition (health, memory, mental alertness, ability to communicate, time schedule, etc.) and (2) the interview location and conditions (disruptions and interruptions, equipment problems, extraneous participants, background noises, etc.)?

b. What evidence is there that the interviewer has (1) thoroughly explored pertinent lines of thought, (2) followed up on significant clues, (3) made an effort to identify sources of information, (4) employed critical challenges when needed, and (5) thoroughly explored the potential of the visual environment, if videotaped?

c. Has the program/project used recording equipment and tapes which are appropriate to the purposes of the work and potential nonprint uses and use of the material? Are the recordings of the highest possible technical quality? How could they be improved?

d. If the interview is videotaped, are lighting composition, camera work, and sound of the highest possible technical quality?

e. In the balance between content and technical quality, is the technical quality good without subordinating the interview process?

PERSPECTIVE

a. Do the biases of the interviewer interfere with or influence the responses of the interviewee?

b. What information is available that may inform the users of any prior or separate relationship of the interviewer to the interviewee?

HISTORICAL CONTRIBUTION

  a. Does the interviewer pursue the inquiry with historical integrity?
  b. Do other purposes being served by the interview enrich or diminish quality?
  c. What does the interview contribute to the larger context of historical knowledge and understanding?

Independent/Unaffiliated Researcher Guidelines

CREATION AND USE OF INTERVIEWS

  a. Has the independent/unaffiliated researcher followed the guidelines for obtaining interviews as suggested in the Program/Project Guidelines section?
  b. Have proper citation and documentation been provided in created works (books, articles, audio-visual productions, or other public presentations) to inform users about the interviews and the permanent location of the interviews?
  c. Do works created include an explanation of the interview project, including editorial procedures?
  d. Has the independent/unaffiliated researcher provided for the deposit of the works created in an appropriate repository?

TRANSFER OF INTERVIEWS TO ARCHIVAL REPOSITORY

  a. Has the independent/unaffiliated researcher properly obtained the agreement of the repository prior to making representations about the disposition of the interviews?
  b. Is the transfer consistent with agreements or understandings with the interviewers? Were legal agreements obtained from interviewees?
  c. Has the researcher provided the repository with adequate descriptions of the creation of the interviews and the project?

d. What is the technical quality of the recorded interviews? Are the interviews transcribed, abstracted, or indexed, and, if so, what is the quality?

Educator and Student Guidelines

Has the educator:

a. become familiar with the "Oral History Evaluation Guidelines" and conveyed their substance to the student?
b. ensured that each student is properly prepared before going into the community to conduct oral history interviews, including familiarization with the ethical issues surrounding oral history and the obligation to seek the informed consent of the interviewee?
c. become knowledgeable with the literature, recording equipment techniques, and processes of oral history, so that the best possible instruction can be presented to the student?
d. worked with other professionals and organizations to provide the best oral history experience for the student?
e. considered that the project may merit preservation and worked with other professionals and repositories to preserve and disseminate these collected materials?
f. shown willingness to share her/his expertise with other educators, associations, and organizations?

Has the student:

a. become thoroughly familiar with the equipment, techniques, and processes of oral history interviewing and the development of research using oral history interviews?
b. explained to the interviewee the purpose of the interview and how it will be used, and obtained the interviewee's informed consent to participate?

c. treated the interviewee with respect?

d. signed a receipt for and returned any materials borrowed from the interviewee?

e. obtained a signed legal release for the interview?

f. kept her/his word about oral or written promises made to the interviewees?

g. given proper credit (oral or written) when using oral testimony, and used material in context?

OHA/American Historical Association Statement on Research Risks

Certain interview research may be governed by the Federal Policy for the Protection of Human Subjects (codified at 45 CFR 46). Such research may require prospective review by an Institutional Review Board (IRB) as well as written informed consent of the interviewee. Additionally, institutions engaged in biomedical and behavioral research are likely to have internal policies that also pertain to interview research. Historians should be cognizant of and comply with all laws, regulations, and institutional policies applicable to their research activities. (February 1996)

Resource Guide

MEDIA LITERACY RESOURCES

The Center for Media Literacy, 4727 Wilshire Blvd., #403, Los Angeles, CA 90010, phone 800-226-9494.

The Media Studies Journal (funded by the Freedom Forum), 580 Madison Ave., 42nd fl., New York, NY 10022.

Center for Commercial-Free Public Education, 1714 Franklin Street, Suite 100–306, Oakland, CA 94612.

Kathleen Tyner, consultant, medialit@sirius.com.

Readings from Marshall McLuhan (*Understanding Media*) and the more contemporary Neil Postman (especially *Conscientious Objections* and *Amusing Ourselves to Death*).

National Writing Project, University of California, 615 University Hall, Berkeley, CA 94720–1670.

The Baffler, Box 378293, Chicago, IL 60637, or visit the Web site at thebaffler.org. This journal has some of the most biting and insightful media criticism today.

FILM AND VIDEO RESOURCES

The following are a few examples of fiction films and documentaries (and their directors) that are useful for classroom activities with *Working*.

Fiction Film

9 to 5 (with Lily Tomlin and Jane Fonda, 1980, dir. Colin Higgins)
Blue Collar (with Richard Pryor, 1978, dir. Paul Schrader)
Matewan (1987, dir. John Sayles)
Modern Times (1936, starring and dir. by Charlie Chaplin)
Norma Rae (with Sally Field, 1979, dir. Martin Ritt)

Salt of the Earth (1953, dir. Herbert Biberman)
Silkwood (with Meryl Streep, 1983, dir. Mike Nichols)

Documentaries

Deadly Deception (dir. Debra Chasnoff)

Harlan County, U.S.A. (1977) and *American Dream* (1989, Barbara Kopple)

Hoop Dreams (1994, Steve James, also a book, *Hoop Dreams*, written by Ben Joravsky, 1995, Turner Publishing)

The Life and Times of Rosie the Riveter (1980, dir. Connie Field)

Roger and Me (1989, dir. Michael Moore)

We Do the Work (The Working Group, 1611 Telegraph Ave., Suite 1550, Oakland, CA 94612. Series of videos for purchase. Phone: 510-268-9675; Fax: 510-268-3606; e-mail: twg@theworkinggroup.org)

Who's Counting? (Marilyn Waring)

ORAL HISTORY WEB SITES

People who gather oral records are historians of the present. Below are a few interesting sites and links they have suggested.

There are innumerable uses for such collections. Using them, students recognize themselves as active historians, finding patterns and sensibilities in multiple constructions of lives.

A simple search of the Internet turns up hundreds of sites. You can find everything from an Inuit self-study project to a high school class that interviewed local World War II veterans. One young man even created a Web page inspired by *Working*, where others can share their job experiences (www.aboutmyjob.com). Invite students to make a query for Oral History in any of the major search engines—Yahoo, Lycos, Hotbot, Excite.

http://dir.yahoo.com/Arts/Humanities/History/ Oral_History/

"1968: The Whole World Was Watching"—includes audio files, transcripts, and edited stories from 30 interviews conducted by high school students around recollections of the events of 1968.

"American Leaders Speak"—recordings from World War I and the 1920 election, from the Library of Congress American Memory Collection.

"California As I Saw It"—first-person narratives of California's early years, 1849–1900.

"Great Speeches from History"—from The History Place.

"Historic Audio Archive"—with Real Audio files of Richard Nixon, John F. Kennedy, Martin Luther King, Jr., and others.

James Cook University Archives of Oral History.

"Jazz Oral History Index"—list of the oral histories on file at the Hogan Jazz Archive at Tulane.

Justin Oral History Center—providing both an avenue to learn the stories of those who have lived history and the opportunity to tell your own.

"Local Heroes"—interviews of World War II veterans from the Bayside area of Melbourne, Australia.

Mississippi Civil Rights Oral History Bibliography—detailed guide to over nine hundred oral history interviews about the civil rights movement in Mississippi.

Navy Oral History Collection—providing Naval, Coast Guard, and Merchant Marine stories, biographies, photographs, and documents.

"Oral History Collections at the Reuther"—transcripts available at the Reuther Library Archives of Labor and Urban Affairs.

"Oral History on Science, Space, and Technology"—an on-line catalog of the contents of oral history projects conducted between 1981 and 1990.

"Oral History Questions"—list from the Gene Pool.

"Oral History Review"—subscription-based publication exploring the recording, transcribing, and preserving of conversations with people who have participated in important developments in modern times.

Rutgers Oral History Archives of World War II.

Social Security Administration Oral Histories—oral history transcripts and archives.

Studs Terkel Interview—An interview with the man who interviews America.

"Tides of Men"—documentary on the lives of gay men in British Columbia from 1936 to the present.

"What Did You Do in the War, Grandma?"—a history of Rhode Island women during World War II. Written by students in the Honors English Program at South Kingston High School.

"Women's Sexuality in WWII Concentration Camps: Tool for Survival, Tool for Oppression"— oral history project. http://www.stg.brown.edu/projects/WWII_Women/.

INSTITUTES AND UNIVERSITY DEPARTMENTS DEALING WITH ORAL HISTORY:

California State University, Long Beach—Oral History Program.

Columbia University—Oral History Research Office.

Indiana University—Oral History Research Center.

Institute of American Indian Studies/South Dakota Oral History Center—the largest oral history collection in the U.S. Topics range from ancient legends and traditional beliefs to recent political and social issues.

University of California, Berkeley Oral History Working Group—contains links to other oral history sites and on-line bibliographies.

University of California, Berkeley, Regional Oral History Office—conducts oral history research about California and the West, located at the Bancroft Library. Contact www.lib.berkeley.edu/banc/roho.

University of Connecticut—Center for Oral History.

University of Hawaii at Manoa Center for Oral History—preserves the recollections of Hawaii's multicultural people through oral history interviews.

University of Southern Mississippi Center for Oral History and Cultural Heritage—interviews with/about Mississippians, index, excerpts (must have sound-card), other guides.

ORAL HISTORY ORGANIZATION

American Gateways Project Settlement House Web Site—curriculum and discussion developed for researching oral histories of New York's Lower East Side and Harlem.

East End Online—nonprofit organization working on an oral history of the town of East Hampton (New York) in the twentieth century.

Oral History Association.

Oral History Project—Oregon history preserved in sound, with tapes, discs, and transcripts spanning 5,500 hours of recorded sound and more than 1,500 individual interviews.

http://www.talkinghistory.org/

The "Talking History" radio show home page, from the Department of History at the State University of New York at Albany, is linked to a weekly radio program focusing on history: ". . . how we recall it, how we preserve it, how we interpret it, how we transform it into myth, and how we pass it on—as teachers, researchers, archivists, museum curators, documentary filmmakers. . . . It is aimed at a nonprofessional audience, and is dedicated to bridging the gap between the history profession and a history-hungry public. . . ." The site will soon feature: "The Myth of the Violent West," "Hot Rain: The Social and Biological History of Radioactive Fallout from American Nuclear Testing in the 1950s and 1960s," and "Female Entrepreneurs: Women and Capitalism in Nineteenth-Century America." The archive of past programs is also on-line, but not all of the programs are available for current viewing.

"Talking History" is now a production, distribution, and instructional center for all forms of "aural" history. Besides the weekly radio program, academic and media specialists affiliated with the center now offer radio production and oral history courses and workshops. In partnership with WRPI-FM (Troy) and the History and MultiMedia Center at the University at Albany—SUNY, the center has initiated a radio production speakers' series and has vastly expanded Internet and Web audio resources at the www.talkinghistory.org site.

Additional production facilities exit at the Department of History, Creighton University (Omaha, Nebraska), and KIOS-FM (Omaha, Nebraska).

Smithsonian Sites

Some of the most important developments in the creation of social histories have been the result of the gathering of oral history, interviewing people who have lived through historic experiences. The oral historian gains information by asking about the everyday experiences as well as the great moments in the lives of people. You can find extensive resources on oral history at the Smithsonian Institution Web site at http://learning.loc.gov/learn/lessons/oralhist/ohhome.html.

About 3,000 oral histories recorded by the Federal Writers' Project are now available online through the American Memory Collection, American Life Histories, 1936–1940. You can refer to these model interviews by consulting the Smithsonian Web site at http://lcweb2.loc.gov/ammem/wpaintro/wpahome.html.

Bibliography

Anderson, Sarah, et al. *Field Guide to the Global Economy*. New York: The New Press, 1999.

Banks, Ann. *First-Person America*. New York: Alfred A. Knopf, 1980.

Baum, Willa K. *Oral History for the Local Historical Society*, 3rd ed. Nashville, Tenn.: American Association for State and Local History, 1969 (3rd ed., 1995).

———. *Transcribing and Editing Oral History*. Nashville, Tenn.: American Association for State and Local History, 1977 (rev. 1991).

Berlin, Ira, Marc Favreau, and Steven Miller, eds. *Remembering Slavery*. Book and audio tape set. New York: The New Press, 1999.

Brecher, Jeremy. *History from Below: How to Uncover and Tell the Story of Your Community, Association, or Union*. New Haven, Conn.: Commonwork Pamphlets/Advocate Press, 1986.

Brouwer, Steve. *Sharing the Pie: A Citizen's Guide to Wealth and Power in America*. New York: Henry Holt, 1998.

Brown, Cynthia Stokes. *Like It Was: A Complete Guide to Writing Oral History*. New York: Teachers and Writers Collaborative, 1988.

Davis, Cullom, Kathryn Back, and Kay MacLean. *Oral History from Tape to Type*. Chicago: American Library Association, 1977 (rev. 1980).

Delaplane, Kristin. *A Gold Hunter: Memoirs of John Berry Hill*. Vacaville, Calif.: Masterpiece Memoirs, 1997.

Doubletake, Fall 1997, Piece on Studs.

Dreifus, Claudia. *Interview*. New York: Seven Stories Press, 1997.

Dunaway, David K., and Willa K. Baum, eds. *Oral History: An Interdisciplinary Anthology*, 2nd ed. Nashville, Tenn.: American Association for State and Local History, in cooperation with the Oral History Association, 1996.

Epstein, Ellen Robinson, and Rona Mendelsohn. *Record and Remember: Tracing Your Roots Through Oral History*. New York: Simon & Schuster, 1978.

Ferris, William. *"You Live and Learn. Then You Die and Forget It All": Ray Lum's Tales of Horses, Mules and Men*. New York: Doubleday, 1992.

Fletcher, William. *Recording Your Family History: A Guide to Preserving Oral History Using Audio and Video Tape*. Berkeley, Calif.: Ten Speed Press, 1989.

Friedman, Thomas. *The Lexus and the Olive Tree*. New York: Farrar, Straus & Giroux, 1999.

From the Old Country: An Oral History of the European Migration to America, with Aldo Salino. New York: Tungue; Toronto, Canada: Maxwell Macmillan, 1994.

Greene, Bob, and D. J. Fulford. *To Our Children's Children: Preserving Family Histories for Generations to Come.* New York: Doubleday, 1993.

Greider, William. *One World, Ready or Not: The Manic Logic of Global Capitalism.* New York: Simon & Schuster, 1997.

Henige, David. *Oral Historiography.* New York: Longman, 1982.

Hoffman, Alice M., and Howard S. Hoffman. *Archives of Memory: A Soldier Recalls World War II.* Lexington: University Press of Kentucky, 1990.

Holmes, Richard. *Footsteps: Adventures of a Romantic Biographer.* London: Hodder and Stoughton, c. 1985.

Hoopes, James. *Oral History: An Introduction for Students.* Chapel Hill: University of North Carolina Press, 1979.

Howe, Barbara J., and Emory L. Kemp, eds. *Public History: An Introduction.* Malabar, Fla.: Krieger Publishing Company, 1986 (rev. 1988).

Howell, Donna Wyant. *I Was a Slave: True Life Stories Told by Former American Slaves in the 1930s.* 4 vols. Washington, D.C.: American Legacy Books, 1995–1996.

Illick, Joseph E. *At Liberty: The Story of a Community and a Generation—the Bethlehem High School Class of 1952.* Knoxville, Tenn.: University of Tennessee Press, 1989.

Ives, Edward D. *An Oral Historian's Work.* Oral History Instructional Videotape. Blue Hill Falls, Maine: Northeast Historic Films, c. 1987.

———. *The Tape-Recorded Interview: A Manual for Fieldworkers in Folklore and Oral History.* Knoxville: University of Tennessee Press, 1980.

Jones, Arnita A., and Philip L. Cantelon, eds. *Corporate Archives and History: Making the Past Work.* Malabar, Fla.: Krieger Publishing Company, 1993.

Kaufman, Sharon R. *The Healer's Tale: Transforming Medicine and Culture.* Madison, Wis.: University of Wisconsin Press, 1993.

Kridel, Craig. *Writing Educational Biography.* New York: Garland Publishing, 1998.

Labrie, Vivian. *Précis de transcription de documents d'archives orales.* Quebec: Institut Quebeçois de Recherche sur la Culture, 1982.

Masumoto, David Mas. *Country Voices: The Oral History of a Japanese-American Family Farm Community.* Del Rey, Calif.: Inaka Countryside Publications, 1987.

———. *Epitaph for a Peach: Four Seasons on My Family Farm.* San Francisco: Harper San Francisco, in association with the Basic Foundation, 1995.

Matters, Marion. *Oral History Cataloging Manual.* Chicago: Society of American Archivists, 1995.

Maurer, Harry. *Strange Ground: Americans in Vietnam, 1945–1975—An Oral History.* New York: Henry Holt, 1989.

Mayer, Henry. *All on Fire: William Lloyd Garrison and the Abolition of Slavery.* New York: St. Martin's, 1998.

McLuhan, Marshall. *Understanding Media: The Extensions of Man.* Cambridge, Mass.: MIT Press, 1994.

Mehaffy, George, Thad Sitton, and O. L. Davis, Jr. *Oral History for Teachers (and Others).* Austin: University of Texas Press, 1983.

Morris, Gabrielle. *Head of the Class: An Oral History of Achievement in Higher Education and Beyond.* New York: Twayne Publishers, an Imprint of Simon & Schuster Macmillan, 1995.

Murnane, Richard J., and Frank Levy. *Teaching the New Basic Skills: Principles for Educating Children to Thrive in a Changing Economy.* New York: Free Press, 1996.

Nuenschwander, John N. *Oral History and the Law.* Pamphlet Series No. 1. Albuquerque, N.M.: Oral History Association, 1985 (rev. 1993).

Oates, Stephen. *Biography As High Adventure.* Amherst, Mass.: University of Massachusetts Press, 1986.

————. *Biography As History.* Waco, Tex.: Mankham Press, 1991.

Pachter, Marc. *Telling Lives.* Washington, D.C.: New Republic Books, 1979.

Patai, Daphne, and Sherna B. Gluck, eds. *Women's Words: The Feminist Practice of Oral History.* New York: Routledge, 1991.

Perks, Robert, and Alistair Thomson, eds. *The Oral History Reader.* New York: Routledge, 1998.

Perry, Theresa, and Lisa Delpit, eds. *The Real Ebonics Debate.* New York: The New Press, 1998.

Portelli, Alessandro. *The Death of Luigi Trastulli and Other Stories: Form and Meaning in Oral History.* Albany: State University of New York Press, 1991.

Postman, Neil. *Amusing Ourselves to Death.* New York: Penguin Books, 1985.

————. *Conscientious Objections.* New York: Vintage Books, 1988.

Read, Peter, ed. *Down There with Me on the Cowra Mission: An Oral History of Erambie Aboriginal Reserve, Cowra, New South Wales.* Sydney and New York: Pergamon Press, 1984.

Ritchie, Donald A. *Doing Oral History.* New York: Twayne Publishers, 1995.

Rosenbluth, Vera. *Keeping Family Stories Alive: Discovering and Recording the Stories and Reflections of a Lifetime.* 2nd ed. Vancouver, B.C.: Hartley & Marks Publishers, 1997.

Saitoti, Tepilit Ole. *The Worlds of a Masai Warrior: An Autobiography.* Berkeley, Calif.: University of California Press, 1988.

Shumway, Gary, and William G. Hartley. *An Oral History Primer.* Published by the authors at Box 11894, Salt Lake City, UT 84147, 1973 (rev. 1983).

Sitton, Thad, et al. *Oral History: A Guide for Teachers (and Others).* Austin: University of Texas Press, 1983.

Stephenson, Shirley E. *Editing and Indexing Guidelines for Oral History.* Fullerton, Calif.: California State University Press, 1978 (rev. 1983).

Stone, Elizabeth. *Black Sheep and Kissing Cousins: How Our Family Stories Shape Us.* New York: Times Books, 1988.

Strom, Margaret Stern. *Facing History and Ourselves, Holocaust and Human Behavior.* Brookline, Mass.: Facing History and Ourselves National Foundation, 1994.

Terry, Wallace. *Bloods: An Oral History of the Vietnam War by Black Veterans.* New York: Ballantine Books, 1984.

Whistler, Nancy. *Oral History Workshop Guide.* Denver: Colorado Center for Oral History, Denver Public Library, 1979.

Wigginton, Eliot, ed. *The Foxfire Book.* Garden City, N.Y.: Anchor Books, 1972.

————. *Foxfire 2.* Garden City, N.Y.: Anchor Books, 1973.

————. *Foxfire 3.* Garden City, N.Y.: Anchor Books, 1975.

Yow, Valerie R. *Recording Oral History: A Practical Guide for Social Scientists*. Thousand Oaks, Calif.: Sage Publications, 1994.

Zeitlan, Steven J., Amy J. Kotkin, and Holly Cutting Baker. *A Celebration of American Family Folk Lore: Tales and Traditions from the Smithsonian Collection*. New York: Pantheon Books, 1982.

Zinsser, William, ed. *Inventing the Truth*. Boston: Houghton Mifflin, 1998.

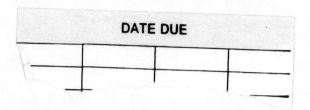

DATE DUE